The Power of a Honeymoon™ Marriage

Discover the authentic blueprint for planning, preparing and sustaining happily-ever-after

WLADIMIR AND ELYSSA JOSEPH

W E Joseph

The Power Of A HONEYMOON™ Marriage

Copyright (c) 2015~WLADIMIR AND ELYSSA JOSEPH

http://WladimirAndElyssa.com

ISBN: 978-0-9963333-4-4 (epub, Kindle/IOS, plain text)

ISBN: 978-0-9963333-5-1 (pbk, plain text, white page interior)

ISBN: 978-0-9963333-0-6 (pbk, black and white photo)

ISBN: 978-0-9963333-1-3 (pbk, color photo)

All rights reserved. No part of this publication may be reproduced, stored in a retrieval system, or transmitted in any form or by any means—electronic, mechanical, digital, photocopy, recording, or any other—except for brief quotations in printed reviews, without the prior permission of the publisher.

Unless otherwise indicated, and verses marked AMP are Scripture quotations taken from the Amplified® Bible. Copyright © 1954, 1958, 1962, 1964, 1965, 1987 by The Lockman Foundation. Used by permission. (www.Lockman.org)

Verses marked NASB are Scripture quotations taken from the New American Standard Bible®. Copyright © 1960, 1962, 1963, 1968, 1971, 1972, 1973, 1975, 1977, 1995 by The Lockman Foundation. Used by permission. (www.Lockman.org)

http://www.WladimirAndElyssa.com

We are deeply thankful for each other, our parents, our supportive community who invests in us, and our loving God, who created the mystery of love and marriage.

We also dedicate this book with love to Jack and LaVonne Atnip, who inspire the world to believe that love can last a lifetime and overcome any obstacle that comes its way. Though the earth crumbles, love remains.

Thank you for demonstrating to the world that a husband and wife can be a bride and groom for life and for showing us that love is like a fine wine: it just gets better with time.

You are loved, and the legacy you created continues to multiply.

Foreword

A few weeks after we came back from our honeymoon in Cancun, we uploaded a video of our wedding, including our exchange of vows, to YouTube. Our friend Linda Potgieter saw our wedding video and she was struck by our vows (Chapter 7 contains Wladimir's vows and Chapter 8 contains Elyssa's vows). Then, motivated by thirteen years of pain in her own marriage, she and her husband reached out to us to find out why and how we wrote such impassioned and grounded vows. They hoped hearing our story would inspire them and give them hope for the future of their marriage. Over Skype, Elyssa and I discussed with them what we had learned and how it impacted and influenced our vows. Unbeknownst to them, we had already undertaken the calling to write this book, and the things we shared with Linda and her husband that day were the unpublished content for this book. Linda and her husband went on to have their marriage rebooted with a re-do of their marriage ceremony. They are now experiencing honeymoon living in their marriage. Below is more of their story as told by Linda.

Wladimir and Elyssa Joseph

Foreword By Linda Potgieter

The very fact that I have the honor of writing this foreword is testimony to the power of Wladimir and Elyssa's influence on marriage.

As a 43-year-old wife, mother, and business woman, I have many blessings to count in my life. Born and raised in South Africa, I started working at 17 and set out to conquer my working world. I have had a fantastic international career, having successfully delivered business projects in 17 countries. I have been headhunted for international positions, I worked on

Nelson Mandela's PR and communications team, I am a business owner, and to date, I still have the privilege of traveling the world working alongside high profile corporate giants.

With all that professional success under my belt, it's fair to say that I became a pretty confident business woman.

However, the same could not be said for my marriage, partly because the skills I used in business did not seem to work so well on my husband!

Born in 1972, to parents aged 17 and 19, I entered the world as the next official generation of divorce. I honor my mother and father as I say that they truly did the best they could with what they had, because they were not afforded a great start in life either, nor were their parents before them. So, my experience of marriage and family life was the color red—a bloody battle.

It was with that red flag that I entered my first marriage in my 20s. After six years of tumultuous dating, I married a really good man and divorced him four months later.

My track record with men over 26 years can be described as a fierce battle for independence. Unfortunately, I have had no flag to raise in celebration and no party afterward to enjoy, because I finally learned that in marriage, when one loses, both lose.

I married my second husband, Jan, in 2002, and he, too, had been exposed to a very independent model of marriage, having divorced his first wife after just six months. With the very best intentions of making ours work, we admit to enduring 13 years of an extremely unhappy, dishonoring, and broken marriage.

I thank God every day that the knowledge that my seven-year-old son would never have survived our divorce kept us hanging in there, clutching with bleeding fingernails onto the wings of prayer and refusing to fail again.

It was with a battle-weary and broken heart, in early 2015, that I watched Wladimir and Elyssa's wedding vows on video. God reminded me instantly of a wedding I had attended in 2012, at which Jan and I both realized that we had entered our marriage as a contract. There was quite simply no characteristic of a covenant to be found between us.

I wept tears of loss, but also of hope, as I replayed their video, confirmation sinking into my heart that there is hope, there is a way.

We immediately asked Wladimir and Elyssa if they would spend a little time with us to share their understanding of marriage, which seemed to run so unbelievably deep for newlyweds! They were tremendously giving of their time, and it was evident that they believed passionately that everyone can enjoy the fruits of a covenant marriage.

We have all heard this word in marriage, even those who are not yet married: unity. But I never understood how unity could come about. Day to day, how do we navigate this relationship and all the challenges it seems to undergo? How do we even celebrate the successes so that we can repeat them again?

It was clear to me that Wladimir and Elyssa had been incredibly intentional prior to getting married. They studied marriage. They explored its purpose. They recognized the blueprint that God had laid out for them. They prepared accordingly, and then they chose to enter marriage with that blueprint in hand.

That same blueprint is getting them from point A to point B, just like satellite navigation. If they get lost, the blueprint reroutes them. If they stumble on a new and rocky road, they know that it's just a matter of time before the blueprint picks up their trail and guides them back onto the right track.

You wouldn't build a house without a plan, would you? Why, then, do we enter the most intimate and sacred human relationship on earth without a concrete plan that comes with a long track record of success? It's crazy. Even if we go for premarital counseling ahead of the big day, it's often a token gesture rather than a decision to undergo essential training and coaching.

Jan and I have Wladimir and Elyssa to thank for impacting us so profoundly, because their wedding inspired us to be remarried. So, on the 3rd of May, 2015, we had the incredible privilege of being married into the covenant that is the glue for our marriage today. We remain deeply grateful to Clint Wolter, who first taught us about covenant marriage, and to Dani Johnson, our coach and mentor, who married us and gave us a new anniversary date!

Since that day, we are experiencing a shift in our mindset about our roles. We feel a bond that we have not felt before. We are finding actual steps that make up a process that is truly strengthening us. My husband is changing before my very eyes. And when we are faced with trials, it's this covenant plan that saves us from ourselves. We find ourselves still on the battlefield, but suddenly we are on the same team—we have realized that we have to fight for our unity!

It is this very image of the warrior wife that Elyssa portrays, and it intrigues me. If you have met her, you know her strength of character. This woman is no pushover! In fact, I would describe Elyssa as striking, passionate, tenacious, driven, influential, beautiful, compassionate, fun, feisty, and probably somewhat demanding. She also has extremely high standards of excellence.

How, then, has this lioness of a woman submitted herself so readily to her new husband's leadership? How has she maintained her influence and her prowess in doing so? The sheer power of her surrender has astounded me. It is abundantly clear that she has a plan. It is equally clear to me that God handpicked Wladimir Joseph to lead and love this woman in life. I am struck by the utter depth and breadth of Wladimir's faith in God, and his action-oriented nature. They are both doers of their faith.

You only need to be in their company for a short while to notice the confidence that they have as newlyweds! It's highly unusual, and extremely appealing. It makes me want what they have.

I want to encourage you, as you read this book: it does not matter where you are in your life or your marriage right now. Don't waste another day on regret; don't lose another day to hopelessness. Make the decision to become a victor in marriage, and no longer a victim.

Let us be teachable and learn from Wladimir and Elyssa, who I believe are called to a powerful union to change the lives of many. Let us expect the honeymoon marriage that they talk about. If they can have it, so can we.

Your decision might be a little risky, but the reward is a marriage revolution!

I am so grateful to God for the hope and grace that He has always shown me. And I am deeply grateful to call Wladimir and Elyssa my friends, two people of the highest caliber who live out their marriage passionately, and change lives wherever they go. Wladimir and Elyssa, thank you for every decision you make daily that proves to me that this adventurous blueprint you talk about is real, delivering results that once I could only dream of.

May God expand the horizons of your beautiful and sacred union to the point of no return!

Linda Potgieter, A wife on a new path

Acknowledgments

Thank you to our parents, Brad and Debbie Williams, and Yves Joseph and Ketly Volcy.

Thank you deeply to Marty and Jenn Rachford, Butch and Diane McCracken, Stephanie Hodges, Bethany Williams, Hans and Dani Johnson, Bob and Kimberly Johnson, Zac and Jacqueline Garver, Kevin and LaToya Hendrickson, Dr. Scott and Kathy Manetsch, and the generous community who supported us in our marriage blast-off.

Thank you Charity Singleton Craig for your editing expertise and helping to make this book a reality

www.charitysingletoncraig.com.

Thank you Trish Roberts for using your internationally renowned photography to capture the book cover art and wedding photos

www.facebook.com/trishroberts01.

Thank you Jeribai Tascoe for your artistic eye, branding expertise and on-point book cover design

www.jeribai.com.

Contents

1 HONEYMOON: FANTASY OR REALITY?   1
    This Is Not Just Another Book on Relationships   2
    The Marriage Landscape Facing Us   3
    The Marriage Landscape Facing You   4
    Radical Stories That Will Change Your Landscape   4
    Daring to Improve the Love Landscape and Set High Standards .   7
    Radical Stories to Help Champion You   8

2 WHAT IF NO BLUEPRINT FOR MARRIAGE EXISTED?   9
    Your $900 Million   9
    Our Spiritual Stories   11
    The Authentic Blueprint is One of a Kind   13

3 THE FIRST MARRIAGE   15
    Does One Plus One Equal One in the "Big Beginning"?   15
    What More Can Matter in This Life and the Life to Come? . .   23
    Blueprints One through Three Summary   29
    What Are the Two Things That Bring Bliss?   31

4 THE FIRST "FAILED" MARRIAGE   33
    What is the "Real" Root Cause of Failure in a Marriage?   33
    Positive Takeaways from the First-Ever Unsuccessful Marriage . .   38
    Blueprint Four Summary   44
    Keeping Marriage War-Zone Free   46

5 THE FIRST FAILED MARRIAGE "REWRITTEN"   47
    Is There a "Real" Successful Husband?   48

Is There a "Real" Successful Wife?	52
Blueprint Five Summary	58
Keeping Marriage Simple	58

6 WHAT IS A HONEYMOON REALLY SUPPOSED TO BE? — 59
Is There a "Real" Definition of "Love"?	59
What Makes Love "For Real"?	66
Blueprint Six Summary	71
Keeping the Pursuit of First Love for God in Marriage	72
An Opportunity to Celebrate Is Awaiting	72

7 THE HONEYMOON-LIVING HUSBAND — 75
How Radical Is Growing in Scripture?	77
God's Blueprint for Premarital Kissing and Sex: Matthew 5:27–30	81
Confident Husbandhood: Ephesians 5:25–29	85
Wladimir's Custom Wedding Vows	86
Confidence for a Husband to Fulfill Vows for a Lifetime	87

8 THE HONEYMOON-LIVING WIFE — 91
Facing Reality: 30 and Still Single	91
The Big Day: The Start of Forever	100
Know What You Are Promising	101
Elyssa's Custom Wedding Vows	101
Confidence for a Wife to Fulfill Vows for a Lifetime	103

9 HONEYMOON LIVING — 107
The Honeymoon Living Blueprint	107
Twelve Guideposts to Honeymoon Living	110
Guideposts Part I: The Battle Plan Against Disinformation	111
Guideposts Part I: Executing the Battle Plan	112
Guideposts Part II: The Battle Plan's Offensive Weapons	115
Guideposts Part II: Executing the Battle Plan	116
Rewards of Becoming Marriage Celebration Experts	126

10 HONEYMOON REVOLUTION: SINGLES ROADMAP — 129
- Your Singles & Dating Revolution Roadmap Activities 129
- Part 2: Slay the Dragon(s) of Your Sexual Past 136
- Part 3: You Are Now Dating 141
- Part 4: You are Single and a Virgin (or a Rededicated Virgin) .. 144
- We Are Built to Have Success in Our Singlehood and Dating .. 151

11 HONEYMOON REVOLUTION: MARRIAGE ROADMAP — 153
- What is Marriage, Again? 154
- Your Marriage Revolution Roadmap Activities 157
- Getting Back to Basics 164
- We Are Built to Have Success in Love and Our Marriage 167

12 HOPE IN A HONEYMOON MARRIAGE REVOLUTION — 169
- The Wedding Day in Action 170
- Wrecks 170
- A Panacea to the World's Ills 174
- Believe for "The Impossible" 177

1 HONEYMOON: FANTASY OR REALITY?

Wife walks in the door after a long day at the office and sets her purse and keys down on the kitchen table, straightens up her ponytail, and heads toward the refrigerator. Husband, who is in the kitchen sipping a glass of sweet tea, notices her and sets down the glass. She starts to walk around him to the refrigerator; he smiles a little as he steps into her path, and he pulls her into his arms with an embrace.

The husband says to his wife, "*I love you more today than I loved you yesterday. I want to love you more. Tomorrow I will love you even more than I love you today.*"

Wife pauses in his arms as she says to him, "*Thank you sweetheart, for your love. Thank you for being the protector of our home and for being a spiritual and physical protector of me.*"

Fantasy Or Reality?

What's your reaction to their dialog? Does it sound fake and unrealistic? Does it sound like a line from a fantasy, fairytale, or romance novel? Is it a statement that exists only in the "honeymoon phase" or in an unrealistic superhero couple?

No. It's not just superhero couples who experience romance like this. Nor is it a line from a fantasy novel. The above exchange actually happened after we got back from our honeymoon in Cancun, about three weeks into day-to-day life.

We (Wladimir and Elyssa) got married in our thirties: the Bride at 32 and the Groom at 38, neither of us previously married. A virgin bride and a "spiritually rededicated virgin" groom. In our relationship, we abandoned very common sentiments about dating, love, romance, and marriage. We first kissed at our wedding ceremony. We started our marriage with an intense study to find clarity on what marriage is and is not. Marriages face many discouraging odds; broken relationships and marriages gone badly are prevalent in our culture. We have experienced a different reality. We experienced a dating relationship filled with fun, love, and honor that we carried into the exceptional marriage that we live today.

Reality

Our experience of confident dating and marriage doesn't have to be for us only or even for a select few. We, too, would have failed in our journey had we not rediscovered an authentic blueprint for dating and marriage. We want to share that blueprint with you.

This Is Not Just Another Book on Relationships

We wanted to write this book as a celebration of marriage—an homage to its wonder and beauty—but the more we analyzed the opposing landscape we faced during our singlehood and dating and now marriage, the more we realized we needed to write this book. This book is now a battle plan, a revolutionary manifesto for combating the incoherence and hostility commonly accepted in our modern day against having confidence in marriage, against marriage as a predictable durable event for the lifetime of the couple, and against marriage as a source of good to the couple and society. Similarly, this book counters the pernicious, comparable battle against singles, especially those with the desire eventually to marry. We are waging war against the belief that singles can't have fulfilling, rewarding relationships during their singlehood, against the deflation of confidence in the hope of marriage, against the promotion of premature intimacy and ill preparation for marriage.

1 HONEYMOON: FANTASY OR REALITY?

We are tackling some hard issues about dating and marriage, ones that we have faced personally and have seen many people face. Yet we have avoided many of the common pains frequent to others. Our hearts break for those who are genuinely hurting, yet we also are inspired to shout from the rooftop that another way is possible. We have a childlike faith that helped us rediscover the authentic blueprint for dating, love, and marriage. We are saddened for those with divorce and similar pain in their past, those currently near the brink of divorce because their marital love has dissipated, or those singles who face comparable pains in their singlehood.

As you begin reading, here is what this book is not: It is not talking about singlehood, dating, or marriage in fluffy, sentimental terms. It is not just for newlyweds or just for the happy-go-lucky. It's not just for couples without children.

What this book is: This book is for those who are hurting. This book is for those who want a clear path, who want a re-do, or who want to do things right the first time around. This book will bring to light a predictable path of a honeymoon marriage long after returning from a honeymoon vacation. It applies to the single person who wants to marry, to the newly married, to the happily married, to the nominally married, or to the married and on the brink of divorce.

The Marriage Landscape Facing Us

The Statistics

Marriage has been a source of great difficulty and challenge to many. These are the statistics on marriage, (assuming US statistics): 41 percent of first marriages end in divorce, 60 percent of second marriages end in divorce, and 73 percent of third marriages end in divorce. That means just about 50 percent of all marriages end in divorce (SOURCE: dailyinfographic.com). Most likely, divorce has affected you or somebody close to you. Maybe your own past or present family circumstance has been affected by divorce and is a source of great pain. We acknowledge your pain in advance, and nothing in this book is meant to add additional pain to your experience, nor are we judging you. Nothing that we say in this book, however difficult or contrary to your understanding of marriage, is intended to add to your pain.

The Marriage Landscape Facing You

What is the marriage landscape you are facing? What is your view on marriage? Is it revolutionary, loving, world changing, and passionate? Or is it a landscape of pessimism? A "welcome to having a ball and chain tied around you" mentality? Or an "enjoy the honeymoon while it lasts" sentiment?

Because of the deluge of negativity surrounding the topic of marriage, we're saving a discussion of the full definition of a honeymoon marriage until chapter three. For the time being, we can say what a honeymoon marriage based on the authentic blueprint is not: It cannot lead to divorce. It cannot lead your marriage relationship to a decrease in love, harmony, or honor over time. It cannot be uninspiring to your neighbors, kids, and others. It cannot be based on passive acceptance of destructive behaviors, or on negative silent agreements like: "we will stick it out until the kids have moved out," or "we will stick it out until we are less financially vulnerable."

Radical Stories That Will Change Your Landscape

The Grooms 9/11 Story

My work was based out of the World Trade Center (Tower One) for three years prior to the 9/11 terrorist attack. It was my first career job out of college, and I loved being part of the caliber and excellence of the global company, Thomson Financial, who had just purchased IBES (International Business Estimates Systems) and was moving this new acquisition around the corner. I was part of a five-or-so skeleton crew still working in Tower One. I am alive to tell this story because of divine promptings I received that morning. I am wrecked by the following event.

It happened during my normal morning routines. Back then I faithfully awoke around five or six o'clock in the morning; got out devotional reading material, my Bible, and a commentary; then prayed and made it out for a thirty-minute door-to-door commute. That morning was just like any other morning, except that it wasn't.

As I woke, I immediately felt a prompting say, *"Go do your laundry."* I pulled the sheets off my bed and tossed them into my laundry pile. Thinking I had appeased the voice, I picked up my Bible to start my devotions.

The prompting came again, *"Go do your laundry this morning."*

I responded back, *"I don't need to; there isn't any emergency, and I still have clean underwear and clothing for today. Besides, I need to get through my Bible and meditation prayer time, and I can't do both my devotions and laundry and still get to work on time."* I proceeded back into my prayer time, but for the only time in my life, I felt as if my prayers would not reach past the ceiling. They fell back down to the ground.

The prompting came again a third time, *"Go do your laundry!"*

I realized that the Lord was dead serious about me listening to Him, and He wanted me to do my laundry, change my routine, and delay going into the office. I got the memo, grabbed my laundry, and headed out of my apartment and around the corner to the laundromat. I made the treks back and forth from my apartment to the laundromat. Before I made my final trip the laundromat, I called into work and notified my co-worker (who sat three chairs from me), that I would be late to the office that morning.

As I took my clothes out of the dryer, the television in the laundromat displayed the news—Tower One of the World Trade Center had just gotten hit. I thought, *"I work there, how odd; what does it mean? Do I have to work today? Do I have to work over time?"* I walked home and turned on the TV, the unfolding news story was still ignorant of what was really happening. Then Tower Two was hit, and it was clear that something was wrong. I hurried and dialed back my co-worker to warn him to get out. The phone system at first dialed but no answer. Then I dialed again and still could not reach him. I got the general voicemail. I realized that I was not going to get through, so I stopped trying and kept watching the news. I saw the collapse of World Trade Center Two and was shocked. Then I saw Tower One collapse. Less than 18 hours prior, I had been eating lunch at the food court just outside Tower One. I was horrified at how close I was to being in these same buildings now collapsing. How could such magnificent buildings get destroyed so easily?

I knew then that the promptings from God were to avert me from being there. I was amazed. I went back into my bedroom, and in utter humility, I cried out with some sheepishness for being at first resistant to hearing God about doing the laundry. I was sheepish and then thankful. I received many calls that day from friends who knew I worked there to find out what happened to me and if I was okay. I could say only that God intervened and told me to go do laundry. I went, did laundry, and never left home. Friends were amazed.

Following the 9/11 tragedy and my path being so graciously redirected, I knew my life was spared for a reason. As I helped the company rebuild their destroyed systems, I renewed my focus and picked back up my seminary application process, sent out my pastoral letter of recommendation (from The Brooklyn Tabernacle), and shortly thereafter got accepted to seminary. Eleven months after 9/11, I headed to Chicago and Trinity Evangelical Divinity School for a Master's Degree (combining a Masters of Divinity and Christian Counseling Psychology). Since 9/11, I have been extremely aware of the premium of being sensitive to God's voice on a daily, moment-by-moment basis, knowing it is the safest way to avert all manner of danger and truly thrive.

Fast forward to October 10, 2013, the day I received a "match" from eHarmony®. Her name was Elyssa. A 31-year-old, six-foot one-inch tall, red-headed, modelesque beauty. I discovered that she loved the Lord and was a virgin who was saving herself for her husband. We were matched for six months, dated six months, engaged for eight weeks and honeymooned for three weeks. We first kissed at the wedding ceremony. The wedding day for us was amazing. It was a dream comes true, and many guests expressed to us that our wedding ceremony was an unparalleled wedding experience for them.

Daring to Improve the Love Landscape and Set High Standards

My 9/11-esque Marriage Promptings

The same sort of promptings that spared my life on 9/11 started recurring in a similar fashion to spare me from a dating and marriage catastrophe. Growing up, I was surrounded by abysmal examples. My parents weren't married and neither of them raised me. The "romance" (dating or marital) relationships in my upbringing environment were rampant with relationship flings, one-night stands, infidelity, and pain. Those in my immediate circle later in life did not have markedly better relationships from the pain, hurt, and brokenness I had seen in my upbringing. As I was about to meet the love of my life, God was bringing to mind that I had choices to make: either go on autopilot and follow society or go find His way for dating and marriage. I sought His face for insights about His plan for dating and marriage and encountered these three promptings:

- Marriage Prompting One – Know the standard that God sets, and use this as motivation and guidance in dating.

- Marriage Prompting Two – Power your marriage from a superior fuel, agape love.

- Marriage Prompting Three – Live an empowered and inspired revolutionary relationship.

This book captures those 9/11-esque warning signs that we heeded when we were approaching marriage. It helps avoid seeds of disaster in dating and marriage and helps to uproot preexisting toxic seeds that have already been sown. It is a blender full of strategy, practical life experience, joy, fun, and a solid foundation for success. Enjoy!

Radical Stories to Help Champion You

An Introduction to The Bride

My parents have been married for thirty-six years. In many regards, my parents' relationship has served as an inspiration for me to set a high standard for my marriage.

I was loved growing up. My story begins in the quaint mountain town of Sonora, California, famous for its history and nature. It was an 1800s Gold Rush Town and borders Yosemite National Park, one of the most famous natural beauties of the world. My great, great, great grandmother was an early pioneer and explorer of Yosemite. I come from a line of independent thinkers and adventures. I was born for adventure and charging a path through unchartered territory. I am the firstborn of six. I have always been a companion to others and a mentor to those around me. Besides having five younger siblings, I was "the big sister" to everybody who needed one. From a young age, I sought to live out God's standards and please Him.

I have lived my whole life having high expectations for myself and cheering for the best in others. I wanted to live life well. I wanted to leave a lasting impact. I have never wanted to live an ordinary life; I have always pushed for the extraordinary. I always wanted to get married. From the age of five, I started laying out my plan of action for finding the man I would marry. Even at five, I knew that he would have the heart of a warrior, and I looked forward to being able to support him and fight beside him.

There are a lot of things that I did right over the next twenty-seven years until I married my husband, but I also had a lot of challenging moments to overcome. It was a process to take a little girl from the mountains and eventually join her to her warrior. This book tells that story. The story of "doing it right," the frustrations along the way, the fear that it wouldn't work, and the victory that ensued. In the next chapter, we are going to tackle what is plaguing marriages and what happens when there is no blueprint for marriage.

2 WHAT IF NO BLUEPRINT FOR MARRIAGE EXISTED?

Your $900 Million

The wedding was a wonderful celebration, and then the groom and bride left their friends and families and headed off for the wedding night.

The groom and bride had dated for several years, and eventually they decided to tie the knot. They were married and headed off for their honeymoon to a lush tropical resort to have some fun and enjoy the waves, culture, music, and some romantic time away. On day three of their honeymoon, the bride was sitting by the pool sipping a margarita and enjoying the sunshine while the groom was in their room taking an afternoon nap in the air conditioning. Her cell phone started to vibrate. She planned to ignore the call because who would be calling her on her honeymoon other than a telemarketer? When she looked down at the phone, however, she saw that it was her beloved grandmother. Worried that something might be the matter, she picked up.

"Hi Grandma."

They chitchatted back and forth for a couple of minutes, and everything seemed fine with Grandma. She talked about the weather, her garden, how pretty her granddaughter looked at the wedding, and how proud she was of her granddaughter. Then grandma's tone changed, and she said, *"I am exercising my will. I am going to give you your inheritance."*

"Oh Grandma. You're sweet, but you don't need to do that. My husband and I both have okay jobs. Things are tight at times, but we make it."

"It's already arranged," Grandma replied. "*I am meeting with the lawyer to finalize the details tomorrow. My dearest granddaughter, I am going to give you a choice; you have a decision to make.*" The bride listened as Grandma continued to explain the details of the will.

As they were wrapping up the call, Grandma said, "*I will be waiting for your decision. Call me back, and let me know what you decide. I need to let the lawyer know your final decision by tomorrow morning.*"

"*Uh, um, okay Grandma.*"

"*Goodbye darling.*"

The bride hung up the phone in utter shock. She stared blankly at it as she tried to process what had just happened. Grandma had given her a choice all right.

She could exercise clause A in her Grandma's will to be awarded $900 million under the condition that she divorce her newly united groom, so that the money would be free from all possible division in a separation of marriage. Also, the conditional clause would be void and null upon any circumventing of it later. Otherwise, she would get $100,000 unconditionally bequeathed to her. She had to make the decision in twenty-four hours or forfeit the conditional award.

The bride thought through the choice she was had been given, "*Wow! $900 million! What am I going to do? Divorce my groom and stay separated from him and get 900 million or stay with him and only get 100,000?*"

※ ※ ※

If you are married, what would you have done if this had happened to you on your honeymoon? Would you respond differently if it happened ten or twenty years into your marriage? Would you choose your spouse over $900 million? How would you respond if you got this offer today?

If you are currently single, how would you respond if you got this same phone call on your honeymoon? Would you choose $900 million over your future spouse? Why or why not?

Obviously, this scenario is highly theoretical, but my bride and I have talked about what we would have chosen if we had been given this same offer during our honeymoon.

We would both forgo $900 million for each other. Why? It is because we have rediscovered the deep understanding of marriage and each other's real worth grounded on the authentic blueprint for marriage. However, we can genuinely say that without building our singlehood, dating and marriage on the blueprint, we wouldn't stand a chance at resisting that pile of cash conundrum! Without learning the blueprint, if we had been presented that offer on our honeymoon, then quickly our honeymoon would have turned into a torturous, nightmarish event. We are blessed to have rediscovered such a source of clarity, guidance, and confidence for marriage! We write these following chapters to help point back to this amazing source.

What is the authentic blueprint? We will unearth it in the upcoming four chapters. Chapter Three dives deeper into why marriage and the rewards and benefits of a spouse are more valuable than $900 million. Chapter Four exposes the one thing that can go wrong in a marriage; it has many different variations, but it is really just one villain. Chapter Five opens up an arsenal of day-to-day resources to bulletproof your marriage and help you experience the fullness of what marriage has to offer. Chapter Six explains the unending love fuel for your marriage, and how to sustain your relationship over time. We provide you with assurance and explain the importance of accountability when you face difficult choices competing with your marriage and spouse. With this guide, it is possible to have a marriage that is ever increasing in love, harmony, intimacy, and durability

Our Spiritual Stories

Each of us on this planet is in a different place in our personal spiritual journey, and we understand that you may not worship the same God we do. We respect where you are in your journey, especially because we, too, have faced tough scenarios, wrestled with unanswered questions, and worked through our own spiritual objections. But in both of our journeys, we found a loving, redeeming, accepting God.

The Bride's Spiritual Journey

I acknowledged the existence of God before I can even remember. I was born into a God respecting Christian home. My parents taught me about God, and our family attended a local church. I gave my heart to Christ as a young child. One standout experience in regards to God occurred when I was about four years old. One of my feet was "pigeon-toed," and I walked with a limp. One night at church, my dad and the assistant pastor prayed for my foot. I was surprised by what I saw as they prayed; I watched as my foot moved from crooked to straight. Since that day, I never walked with a limp again! That encounter left quite an impression.

In my growing up years, the reality of life hit. I had many spiritual frustrations to work through. I struggled with how to process the hypocrisy I saw in "Christians." I had many unanswered questions. I had seen loved ones suffer and die, and I heard the arguments of science and culture. I knew the Bible stories, and I had all the "right answers," but I struggled for years with why the reality of what was in front of me seemed so different from the teachings of the Bible. It didn't make sense to me. If Jesus was who the Bible said that He was, if God the Father was who the Bible said that He was, then there had to be more. There had to be answers. I could rationally argue away the existence of God, but every time I did, a little voice reminded me of the night as a preschooler that I watched my crooked foot go straight. I couldn't forget that one reality.

Just months after I finished high school, I found myself in a standoff with God. I realized I had a choice: a choice to believe He was who He said He was or to run away from Him. I ran toward Him, and over the next few years, I found Him in radical, new proportions. He really is who He says He is. He heals, He loves, and He sets the captives free.

The Groom's Spiritual Journey

My story started nine years before 9/11 during my senior year of high school. While returning home on the 14th Street L Line train in Manhattan, someone gave me a pamphlet about God. The pamphlet basically said, "*Hey,*

2 WHAT IF NO BLUEPRINT FOR MARRIAGE EXISTED?

there is an amazing boon you can be experiencing at this time. This is unlike any promise made by politicians or in an infomercial." It went on to say, "*Having a relationship with your Creator completes your purpose and gives significance to your existence.*" Furthermore, "*no human person, no matter who they claim to represent, should ever be permitted to sully the truth about living in an active relationship with your Creator.*" That's it.

I accepted the invitation, and my life changed significantly. Especially noticeable were the answers I found to the deep-seated questions about my reason for being. Since then, God has never been marred in my eyes. No matter how perplexed I become about religious people or culture, no matter how confused or disappointed I was about those who profess belief in God, I am never disappointed in God Himself.

We Acknowledge Your Pain

Few topics seem to bring more fights and pain to the table than "God" and "marriage." We acknowledge that the discomfort you may feel about the topics surrounding God and marriage is real. We are not here to trivialize it. We are deeply saddened about any pain you have experienced, whether that pain is about God, your singlehood, your current marriage relationship, past abandonments, rejections, or abuses. We don't intend to cause you any further pain. Quite the contrary: we are here to champion you toward hope and healing.

The Authentic Blueprint is One of a Kind

For what follows in these chapters, we make no apologies. Here's why.

Reason one. Throughout this book, we appeal to the blueprint of marriage that we didn't invent. This is a blueprint built from the most fundamental and earliest instruction on marriage in the Bible, the union of Adam and Eve.

Reason two. We are both relatively young (70-years combined living life solo) and first time newly married, but our confidence is not in ourselves, nor our willpower, nor our genius reinvention of marriage. Rather, Psalms 119:97-100 (a Jewish and Christian text) says (paraphrased), *"Those who love God's words and frequently meditate on or learn from them will have better insight than all their more schooled contemporaries because of the superior insights found from the source of God's words."*

Reason three. We both have experienced the extraordinary benefits of following the blueprint while dating. Our courtship was fun even in the midst of walking through tough life experiences together. The inspiration for the bride to remain a virgin for thirty-two years was because of the motivation and foundation she found in the blueprint. The groom kept their relationship pure and honored her during our dating because he, too, found the guidance for leading a relationship based on God's standards. We have radical and excellent results from the authentic blueprint. We have an incredible love for each other built up throughout our dating relationship and in our marriage. The ongoing honeymoon and bliss we experience is explicitly grounded in our whole-hearted pursuit after God's blueprint for marriage.

The Blueprint Unleashed In the Next Three Chapters

What follows in the next chapter is Part One of the authentic blueprint for marriage. Although a fairly well-known story, it's rarely used for its practical benefit to married people or for its hope for the person who wants to get married. However, this story describes a dynamic that will get you pumped about marriage, leading into the honeymoon, and long after the honeymoon vacation is over, even fifteen, thirty, fifty, and seventy-five years into your marriage. This first part of the blueprint is like triple platinum jet fuel to your love or singles life. We will not hide one iota of how we came to our conclusion about the full blueprint. Instead, we put the same information we found and used from the blueprint at your fingertips. Then you can look at the original source we used to gain our radically positive results, and draw from it the answers you are seeking.

3 THE FIRST MARRIAGE

In this chapter, we will cover the first marriage, the marriage of Adam and Eve. Although it's a fairly well known story, it's rarely considered to have a practical benefit to the married person or the person who hopes to get married. The first marriage is part one of the authentic blueprint that creates positive hope in marriage.

Had we not been steeped ourselves in the Scriptures during the year leading to our marriage, we would have come up with our own blueprint for marriage. It would have been based on our own wisdom and experience. Or maybe it would have been based on our culture's standard for marriage. However, Scripture impacted our hearts and minds and showed us God had plans for marriage. He built into it joy and pleasures that were predictable rather than elusive or temporarily confined to just a wedding night or honeymoon. God ordained marriage to be good. This is distinctively different from the unpredictability of a marriage where those in it invent the marriage design along the way.

Does One Plus One Equal One in the "Big Beginning"?

We believe marriage can be beautifully lived out with confidence and a revolutionary spirit. However, those who are or will be married need the right information from the authentic marriage blueprint to live their marriage successfully!

Your "One Plus One" By the Authentic Blueprint Activities

ACTIVITY INSTRUCTIONS

The rest of this chapter is in an interactive workbook format.

How? We will frequently prompt the readers to pause and observe, answer questions, brainstorm, or invite them to check out external tools to get further help. Also note: when an activity references scripture passages, we encourage you to follow along in The Scriptures, using your Bible or one online. In most activities, we will use The Amplified® Bible Translation, (AMP). Then we will make a summary observation of the scripture passage verse by verse, which will be labeled "WEJ-Paraphrase."

Why? FIRST, so you the reader can gain the maximum benefit through participation. **SECOND**, to permit later interactive activities to be-added-on, and accelerate the benefits you gain from the material. **THIRD**, to permit a bridge to have later live interaction with authors and teams dedicated to championing your success in singlehood, marriage, and love by God's design. **FORTH**, as you work through the activities below, you may find yourself wanting to go deeper and explore more.

Additional tools and support at:
www.ThePowerOfAHoneymoon.com/phmtools

Reading Activity 3.1: Genesis 1:20–2:25

Read the creation and first marriage story from Genesis 1:20 – 2:25. Then, look at some key passages with us below and consider them in their original context and emphasis and timeless impact.

AMP (Gen. 2:7)

> Then the Lord God formed man from the [a] dust of the ground and breathed into his nostrils the breath or spirit of life, and man became a living being.

WEJ-Paraphrase (Gen. 2:7)

God created Adam from dirt and the breath of God. Adam is forever dependent on God for the breath of life that empowers him.

Each person is built with an external dependency on God to thrive and to have a purpose. (Gen. 2:7)

AMP (Gen. 2:15)

And the Lord God took the man and put him in the Garden of Eden to tend and guard and keep it.

WEJ-Paraphrase (Gen. 2:15)

God first creates Adam and places him in his role of responsibility; Eve is not yet created, and hence Adam is the head and leader by God's design to steward this massive calling and command from God. Adam's leadership remains intact when God later completes Adam with Eve.

We are completed to thrive as stewards for God and God gives each person a purpose to fulfill. (Gen. 2:15, 16-17)

AMP (Gen. 2:18)

Now the Lord God said, it is not good (sufficient, satisfactory) that the man should be alone; I will make him a helper (suitable, adapted, complementary) for him.

WEJ-Paraphrase (Gen. 2:18)

God also created in Adam an external dependency on Eve so that Adam could put into practice the relational and intelligence attributes that God built into him. These are the same attributes displayed in the Triune Godhead of Father and Son and Holy Spirit.

Without Eve being built for Adam, he would be incomplete to fulfill a mandate given to him.

Adam is incomplete or insufficient to steward certain mandates God wants for him to steward. Adam or the one who is single is complete until God gives a mandate necessitating him or her to need marriage. Then, at that moment, God will similarly provide the complementing companion to fulfill the secondary agenda.

God ensures each person is adequately completed to have what is needed to live out God's unique purpose for him or her. (Gen. 2:18, 21-22; 1:28)

AMP (Gen. 2:20)

And Adam gave names to all the livestock and to the birds of the air and to every [wild] beast of the field; but for Adam there was not found a helper meet (suitable, adapted, complementary) for him.

WEJ-Paraphrase (Gen. 2:20)

Adam gave names to the land and sky animals, but then he observed none of them could complete him, and he had no suitable helper.

"Not suitable" means there was no one like Adam who could help him. Since Adam was made in God's image and God is three persons in one, to be like God means Adam needed to live in relationship with another who is both like him and able to match his gifts with her own (not just animals or birds).

God already knew that Adam was incomplete, and it was infinitely genius of God to let Adam come to this same conclusion on his own before God gave him an external dependency on Eve. Adam might never have accepted Eve as a completion to him if he had not recognized that he was lacking a suitable helper "a helpmate" far different than land or sky animals.

What Adam Could Not Do Alone:

3 THE FIRST MARRIAGE

- Fully bearing God's image (Gen. 1:27)

- Living in community, like the relationship of the Trinity

- Multiplying or procreating (Gen. 1:28)

What Adam Could Do Alone:

- Adam was able to tend the garden and exercise dominion over the animals and the earth (Gen. 1:26, Gen. 2:20). *(Below is more explanation to what Adam could do alone.)*

Are Singles *"Not suitable"* Until They Are Married?

Answer: No. There is a three-part answer.

1) Adam was single long enough to perform tasks by himself, Gen. 2:20.

In hindsight, joining the creation story and the events following the first marriage fall, and throughout Scripture, a single, male or female is a complete person in God's vantage. *The only vantage that matters, since God gets to have the final say in Revelation.* Adam prior to Eve portrays a life of a single person. Adam, while single, God gave him the mandate to tend the garden (Gen. 2:15-16). Likewise, God will give a single person mandates, and God will hold him or her accountable.

2) People after Adam, Throughout The Scriptures Were Given Life Callings to Be Single

Later after the fall of Adam and Eve, we see that people are called to be single for part or their whole life. Therefore, they are complete in God's sight until God pronounces He has a secondary calling for him or her, which necessitates being married along with that calling/purpose/mission. God knows best and makes this decision, not the person.

3) Singles Are As Complete As A Married Couple

The single person (that is engaged in doing God's work) is as complete as the married couple doing God's work. God is who dictated when Adam wasn't complete to fulfill a particular agenda of God.

Bonus: Good News For Singles, God Will Not Neglect

Singles are meant to thrive in God's work and never to have a complex of inadequacy and incompletion while they are single. Only God gets to deem a single person incomplete when He gets them ready for a marriage that will further (complete) His work. Conversely, the single person not actively involved in doing God's work will find it extremely difficult to be sure if God has a work for him or her that necessitates being married.

AMP (Gen. 2:21)

In addition, the Lord God caused a deep sleep to fall upon Adam; and while he slept, He took one of his ribs or a part of his side and closed up the [place with] flesh.

WEJ-Paraphrase (Gen. 2:21)

After Adam became aware of his need for a helper, God gave him both a downgrade and then a completion. The downgrade included losing part of his side (something significant to him). The downgrade makes Adam forever inadequate and codependent at a significant, discernible level. However, Adam's completion through Eve was the ideal of God for a completed human creation.

God transformed Adam from being "not suitable" to being "suitable" to fulfill His mandate. Eve's creation was not an enhancement to Adam or a mutation of him. Adam and Eve are not an excess to or appendage of each other. They are now essential to each other. Here the creation story tells of the physical and spiritual tie of oneness between a husband and a wife. The creation story also suggests a correlation to Eve being the by-product of Adam's living tissue just as from then on all human life would come from the living tissue of a woman's womb.

The Lord caused a deep sleep for Adam in order to create Eve. In that moment, the human race extended to include both male and female, but it was more than that. By using Adam's rib, God forged a physical interdependence between the two that Adam could not have experienced through any other means.

AMP (Gen. 2:22)

In addition, the rib or part of his side, which the Lord God had taken from the man, He built up and made into a woman, and He brought her to the man.

WEJ-Paraphrase (Gen. 2:22)

Eve completes Adam, and this is *The First Marriage*. Fast forward through to Revelation, the life after earth is portrayed as another wedding, *The Final Marriage*.

- *² And I saw the holy city, the new Jerusalem, descending out of heaven from God, all arrayed like a bride beautified and adorned for her husband; ³ Then I heard a mighty voice from the throne and I perceived its distinct words, saying, See! The abode of God is with men, and He will live (encamp, tent) among them; and they shall be His people, and God shall personally be with them and be their God. (Revelation 21:2-3, AMP)*

Adam and Eve are built to fulfill a unique mandate for their marriage union. Humanity is filled with fabulous attributes unparalleled among the animals or plants or any other created things.

During the Genesis creation story, God did not create anything with His meticulous hands-on attention aside from Adam and Eve.

AMP (Gen. 2:24)

Therefore a man shall leave his father and his mother and shall become united and cleave to his wife, and they shall become one flesh.

WEJ-Paraphrase (Gen. 2:24)

This verse tells us that the marriage story of Adam and Eve is mystically replicated every time a marriage occurs. The same comprehensive joining and dependency happens in every God ordained marriage. The new couple leaves behind their birth families and is united together as a new family unit.

To go deeper on section 3.1,
Visit www.ThePowerOfAHoneymoon.com/phmtools

Writing Activity 3.2:

- 3.2.1. After reviewing the harmony and the blissful beginning that Adam and Eve experienced in their relationship, are there practical benefits this story can offer for your marriage or your future marriage? Alternatively, for the single, male or female, what blazing clarity does this passage bring to your daily life?

_____

_____

- 3.2.2. From your reading, is there a way Adam could have been complete? Or, is there a way Eve could have been built and have been even a more "suitable helper" to Adam? Please explain your answer.

_____

_____

- 3.2.3. Did you see the deep dependency and inseparability that Adam has with God, being indwelt with the breath of God? For the single, or married, what does this mean to you? Additionally, what does the deep dependency and inseparability between Adam and Eve say to you?

_____

_____

- 3.2.4. How might this clarity for the married, help you to help your spouse each day? For the single, how might this clarity bring help from The Lord for you each day?

_____

_____

What More Can Matter in This Life and the Life to Come?

Our wedding was a wonderful celebration, and then we left our friends and families and headed off for the wedding night.

To our great delight, our consummation was not just a physically intimate act with finite consequences. Instead, our connectedness was a heavenly joining.

In Matthew 19:6, referring to the creation of Adam and Eve, Jesus says, "So they are no longer two, but one flesh. What therefore God has joined together let no man put asunder (separate)." Not only does Jesus treat the story as sacred, nowhere in the Bible are we told that this story of Adam and Eve is a just a figure of speech or poetic illustration or fairytale. Moreover, it is certainly not just a nice story for wedding ceremonies.

Just like Eve was bone of bone to Adam, so too I felt an external dependency on Elyssa. When I viewed our union in light of the heavenly reality, it was easy for me to cherish her. Similarly, she is freed to abandon herself to me as her "Adam" and to allow our new union to supersede her single identity, no matter how great it was in and of itself. Hence, the overflowing passion I had and still have for my bride is powered by the Bible story found in Genesis 1-3. Relentless passion is built into God's marriage blueprint, the same passion I am demonstrating for Elyssa. In addition, the boundless love I have for her comes from what God says she is to me and I am to her.

God intended marriage to be amazing, and we are experiencing it, accepting it, and allowing for no other definition of marriage.

The story of creation is that God creates Adam, but for what? The start of marriage is God joins Adam and Eve, but for what purpose? The single person is asking one of the greatest questions they can ask, when they ask, *"For what purpose did You, God, create me, as a single, and for this duration of singlehood in my life?"* Similarly, the married can ask, *"For what purpose did You, God, join me and my spouse together?"*

For multimedia companion on this section #3.3.1,
  Visit www.ThePowerOfAHoneymoon.com/phmmedia

Your "What Is Your Ultimate Life and Marriage Mandate" By the Authentic Blueprint Activities

Reading Activity 3.3: Genesis 1:26–1:28, 2:25

Now read the story surrounding the ultimate mandate for life and marriage, Genesis 1:26–1:28, 2:25. Then, look at some key passages with me below and consider them in their original context, emphasis and timeless impact.

AMP (Gen. 1:26)

> God said, Let Us [Father, Son, and Holy Spirit] make mankind in Our image, after Our likeness, and let them have complete authority over the fish of the sea, the birds of the air, the [tame] beasts, and over all of the earth, and over everything that creeps upon the earth.

> **WEJ-Paraphrase (Gen. 1:26)**

God made humankind patterned after His own image and likeness and based on His attributes as Triune God. None of these qualities is found in the land animals, fishes, or birds. Only Adam received the breath of God (Gen. 2:2). God's spirit lives in humanity and forms them into spiritual beings. Because God gave Adam and Eve His own image, they also can create from their choices or will. They are not robots operating without a "free will." Instead, God positioned them with great guidance in the essence of their identity (God's image bearers). God gives nothing without holding the receivers to account. Therefore, God positioned Adam, His image bearer, in the Garden of Eden as a steward. Adam had a choice to live out his God-given abilities to tend the garden, and then to exercise dominion over the animals and the earth.

Summary: God created Adam, and then later completes him with Eve, to perform stewarding tasks in the world; the two have a purpose to fulfill together.

AMP (Gen. 1:27)

So God created man in His own image, in the image and likeness of God He created him; male and female He created them.

WEJ-Paraphrase (Gen. 1:27)

God made humans as spiritual beings, just as God is Spirit.

AMP (Gen. 1:28)

In addition, God blessed them and said to them, Be fruitful, multiply, and fill the earth, and subdue it [using all its vast resources in the service of God and man]; and have dominion over the fish of the sea, the birds of the air, and over every living creature that moves upon the earth.

WEJ-Paraphrase (Gen. 1:28)

Adam and Eve receive God's blessing, along with instructions for their joint work as husband and wife. God's instructions are the same as commands. He holds the recipients accountable as shown later (Gen. 3:17) in how they receive a demotion when their marriage union fails to steward part of its purpose. Their newfound purpose as a couple is to:

–**Be fruitful**, to use the talents endowed to them individually and as a couple; also including singles.

–**Reproduce**, to have children to pass on God's mandate. For Adam and Eve, this meant having literal children. For most married couples, the same is true, they have children that they birth and parent. Additionally God's heart is that not one of His kids would be orphaned or feel all alone. Singles and married alike can adopt, spiritually parent, and love others in such a way that they invest into others and "reproduce" as God gives them opportunity.

–**Subdue the earth**, to care for the animals and to maximize the earth's resources in order to provide for the populated earth in a balanced way.

These mandates are timeless and extend to later married couples, or the single person.

AMP (Gen. 2:25)

And the man and his wife were both naked and were not embarrassed or ashamed in each other's presence.

WEJ-Paraphrase (Gen. 2:25)

In the verse, the summary description also defines the timeless design of the first and all later marriages. God sets the standard for Adam and Eve to live out the completion of each other (also now known as marriage). God built a marriage to be without the barrier or hindrance of shame and embarrassment between spouses. God, their maker, is an integral part of the union in a spiritual connection and hence no similar barrier (of **shame** and embarrassment) is permitted between them and God. The spouses are built to have with each other a "**nakedness**" or trust and transparency along being "**not ashamed**" or without inadequacy issues between each other that causes them to be in full unity and harmony with one another.

<u>Summary</u>: The couple is enjoying life, sharing everything.

Recap and a Glance of Genesis Major Creation Events with Timeless Ongoing Impact

- Gen. 2:7 - Adam is specially hand-made from dust and the life and breath of God.

- Gen. 2:15-17 - God gives Adam a responsibility to protect the garden where the temptation would later occur. (Later in verse 21-22, God builds Eve, the perfect suitable helper, and unites them through the perfect interdependent marriage union to achieve God's goal for them.) *The pattern is set for the single life. A single life is completed for the time being that he or she is completely/suitably accomplishing God's delineated purpose for the single person. If God appends an additional mandate to the single person, then He will also deem the person as a single/alone is "not suitable" to fulfill the new mandate. Finally, God will initiate building the suitable companion to join to the person.*

- Gen. 2:18, 21 – Verse 18, Adam agrees with God that he is incomplete without a suitable helper; Verse 21, Adam has a significant part removed from him, which makes him incomplete and ready to receive God's complement through Eve.

- Gen. 2:22 - Eve is made from the living tissues of Adam with a "special inextricable formula" in order to be forever fulfilled through conjoining with Adam. Adam and Eve are joined or married together for a purpose, which Adam was not "suitable" to fulfill as a single. *The pattern is set for marriage. Marriage is the completion of two to fulfill a purpose God delineates.*

Writing Activity 3.4:

- 3.4.1. After reviewing these additional verses from the Adam and Eve story, what do you think your source of motivation should be as a married couple? Alternatively, for the single, male or female, what blazing clarity does this passage bring to your daily life?

    _____
    _____

- 3.4.2. As a married person, did you see the firm mandate by God to live interdependently with each other? Or, for the single, did you see the deep dependence on God's breathed breath in you? What is the mandate given particularly to you, as a single, or to your marriage, as a spouse?

    _____
    _____

- 3.4.3. Whether married, or single, what would motivate you and help bring you more clarity in how to fulfill your God given mandate on a daily basis?

    _____
    _____

- 3.4.4. How can the original creation story bring fun, satisfaction, freshness and other good things into your daily life?

3 THE FIRST MARRIAGE

_____

_____

To go deeper on section 3.4,
Visit www.The*PowerOfAHoneymoon*.com/phmtools

✳ ✳ ✳

Blueprints One through Three Summary

A summary of Blueprint I is found in Genesis 2:15.

We are <u>**exquisitely completed**</u> <u>**to thrive as stewards**</u> for God.
   Part 1 of 3, Each person is built with an external dependency on God to thrive and to have a purpose. (Gen. 2:7)
   Part 2 of 3, God gave each person a purpose to fulfill. (Gen. 2:15, 16-17)
   Part 3 of 3, God ensured each person is adequately completed to have what is needed to live out God's unique purpose for him or her. God takes it upon Himself to pronounce the judgment of incompletion, "**It is not good that the man should be alone,**" and He subsequently rectifies what is needed to make the person **suitable**. (Gen. 2:18, 21-22; 1:28)

A summary of Blueprint II is found in Genesis 2:7, 24.

<u>**Our exquisite completion and entering into the future begins after we make a significant break from the past.**</u>
   Part 1 of 2, Adam and Eve were joined without there being unresolved spiritual roadblock issues from their past that would be the cause of the doom to their future. Adam lived in a state of dependency on God prior to being joined to Eve. Similarly, prior to any individual being joined to their calling or helpmate, there is a prerequisite.
   A readiness to pursue God's calling necessitates an ability to discern God's invitation into that calling. An individual discerning his or her life's calling or taking confident beginning steps to commence that calling seems correlated with

the depth of spiritual freshness in their relationship with God. To be optimally pushed into new places in your future calling, each person thrives living **naked, not ashamed and not hiding from God.** *(Gen. 2:7, 25; 3:8)*

Part 2 of 2 (The Wedding Day Prerequisite and The Ceremony, covered in chapter 12), The Wedding Day Event can make everything brand new for the couple, if there is a commitment from them to start by **leaving** behind all possible hindrances that would interfere with their joining and calling together; this may also include hindrances from soul ties from past relationships, or from family-oriented generational issues, or any ties with a person or thing that have an oppressive impact on the individual.

God created each married couple to receive a monumental fulfillment through the dependency on his or her spouse. God forges each married couple into an inseparable spiritual oneness that mirrors the physically intangible oneness that started in the first marriage, the joining of Adam and Eve. The intangible physical oneness begins during the marriage ceremony, through their **leaving** their pasts behind before they can cleave together. *(Gen. 2:21–25)*

A summary of Blueprint III is found in Genesis 2:7, 22.

Our exquisite completion comes standard with bountiful blessings.

Part 1 of 3, God built the external dependency for each person on Him so they could experience a rewarding connectedness and relationship with Him. Each person thrives living **naked, not ashamed and not hiding from God.** *(Gen. 2:7, 25; 3:8)*

Part 2 of 3 (The Wedding Day Consummation), in modern times God continues to forge each married couple into an inseparable spiritual oneness that mirrors the physically intangible oneness that started in the first marriage, the joining of Adam and Eve. The intangible physical oneness begins during the marriage ceremony through the bride and groom leaving their past individual identity, and becoming a new identity by the **cleaving** together that the couple does on their marriage bed. *(Gen. 2:21–25)*

Part 3 of 3, God's design for each couple is to live with each other **naked, not ashamed, and not hiding from God.** *(Gen. 2:7, 25; 3:8)*

What Are the Two Things That Bring Bliss?

When we read these passages from Genesis, we found that the external motivations when compared to the biblical motivation for living in harmony with each other paled in comparison. Genesis gives us the good news about the marriage we all can have. God has built into marriage "oneness" within the start of the marriage as part of the design. The harmonious union and inter-dependency are standards to begin and grow higher; it will last if the spouses don't put hindrances of shame and embarrassment between each other. The oneness that God designed is motivation enough for guarding against foreign objects, in particular, the lies of the enemy seeking to derail marriage harmony.

However, if we needed another motivation to live in harmony with our spouses other than its sheer benefits to the soul, then another motivation is that God is holding each of us accountable for the way we steward His design of our oneness, and our relationships, our talents, our children, and the earth. Therefore, our motivation needs to align with God's standard.

For the single, male or female, the above passages give the good news of a loving Lord. He created you to have fellowship with the God of the universe. He gives a mandate or mission He deemed uniquely meaningful and rewarding for your life and His grand plans.

The single, male or female, is *complete* when single. God does not create incomplete persons, He creates us, to have what we need for when we need to fulfill His purpose. Living in relationship with God brings full completion and fulfillment. When God adds another agenda to the single person's life that merits marriage, God will give to the single, the suitable companionship he or she needs *to complete* the calling from Him suitably.

The next chapter introduces the one and only thing that can go wrong in marriage. The one thing is never your spouse but instead the one common enemy.

4 THE FIRST "FAILED" MARRIAGE

In this chapter, we will cover part two of the first marriage, when Adam and Eve turned from God's instructions and were foiled by the serpent.

I (Wladimir) was brought into the world by parents who were not married, and my parents did not raise me. In addition, the romantic relationships in the homes of my upbringing were short-term relationships, filled with infidelity and pain. Usually, the pain was caused by the arbitrary definition of dating and marriage that my family members held.

As I headed into my own marriage, I knew I could not rely on the examples of my past. In fact, I wanted to avoid 98 percent of what I observed around me while growing up. Similarly, since the account of Adam and Eve is a real story with real consequences, I sought for insight from The Lord and learned what not to do, in order to avoid their same failures. Elyssa and I hope you will learn these lessons, too and avoid unnecessary pain in your own life.

In the next chapter, we will offer several solutions to the major problems Adam and Eve encountered. But first, we have to understand what went wrong.

What is the "Real" Root Cause of Failure in a Marriage?

The disharmony and failures Adam and Eve experienced in their marriage is able to be isolated to how Adam and Eve unsuccessfully discerned their common enemy. Their common enemy, Satan, tempted them but their actions solely determined the tragic outcome of the story.

The enemy is not the root cause to failure in marriage. He is only a foe for which the Christian married or single have the supreme advantage to defeat. The root cause failure originates in how effective the Christian leverages the supreme advantage they are given to overcome the one foe to a rewarding marriage or a thriving singlehood. The first marriage failure gives guidance on what not to do. Do you want to find out what not to do?

Your "What To Never Ever Do In Marriage" By the Authentic Blueprint Activities

ACTIVITY INSTRUCTIONS

The rest of this chapter is in an interactive workbook format.

How? We will frequently prompt the readers to pause and observe, answer questions, brainstorm, or invite them to check out external tools to get further help. Also note: when an activity references scripture passages, we encourage you to follow along in The Scriptures, using your Bible or one online. In most activities, we will use The Amplified® Bible Translation, (AMP). Then we will make a summary observation of the scripture passage verse by verse, which will be labeled "WEJ-Paraphrase."

Why? **FIRST,** so you the reader can gain the maximum benefit through participation. **SECOND,** to permit later interactive activities to be-added-on, and accelerate the benefits you gain from the material. **THIRD,** to permit a bridge to have later live interaction with authors and teams dedicated to championing your success in singlehood, marriage, and love by God's design. **FORTH,** as you work through the activities below, you may find yourself wanting to go deeper and explore more.

<u>Additional tools and support at:</u>
www.ThePowerOfAHoneymoon.com/phmtools

Reading Activity 4.1: Genesis 2:15–3:19

Read about the disharmony and failures Adam and Eve experienced in their marriage in Genesis 2:15–3:19. Then, look at some key passages with us below and consider them in their original context and emphasis and timeless impact.

4 THE FIRST "FAILED" MARRIAGE

AMP (Gen. 2:15)

And the Lord God took the man and put him in the Garden of Eden to tend and guard and keep it.

WEJ-Paraphrase (Gen. 2:15)

God first creates Adam and places him in his role of responsibility; Eve is not yet created, and hence Adam is the head and leader by God's design to steward this massive calling and command from God. Adam's leadership remains intact when God later completes Adam with Eve.

AMP (Gen. 2:16)

And the Lord God commanded the man, saying, You may freely eat of every tree of the garden.

WEJ-Paraphrase (Gen. 2:16)

When God creates Eve from Adam, He brings her to Adam in the garden. Together Adam and Eve represent the image of God. Eve is not a second-class citizen or an afterthought in creation, she is the wife (or completion) of Adam. Eve is made to be alongside Adam to fulfill God's agenda delineated to Adam. Adam and Eve's significance is not in the order of their creation or their uniqueness in their male or female sex. Instead, they have an important mandate to fulfill together and they are built as a perfect union to fulfill their calling.

Eve is Adam's companion, and while she has a major role to play, ultimately she is not the one that God holds the most responsible when the fall occurs. Adam is held most responsible since God built him as the leader in the marriage union.

AMP (Gen. 2:17)

But of the tree of the knowledge of good and evil and blessing and calamity you shall not eat, for in the day that you eat of it you shall surely die.

WEJ-Paraphrase (Gen. 2:17)

God will hold Adam accountable to obey the calling and direction God has set for him, even if he is tempted or coerced to veer off course by his soulmate, Eve. The reward at stake for Adam, and later for Eve when she is created, is that they get to enjoy the complete provision God has given them in the delightful garden. Implied in Adam's leadership role is the responsibility to guide and protect his soon-to-be-formed companion, Eve, so that she is clear about the calling Adam received and so that she relies on her relationship with God and Adam to withstand any compromises to their calling. Likewise, Adam can rely on God to help him resist any temptation to stray from the calling God gave him. Failure was not inevitable in God's marriage blueprint. In fact, God gave Adam and Eve everything they needed to ensure success.

AMP (Gen. 2:18)

Now the Lord God said, It is not good (sufficient, satisfactory) that the [Adam] should be alone; I will make him a helper (suitable, adapted, complementary) for him.

WEJ-Paraphrase (Gen. 2:18)

Prior to creating Eve, God specifies the role she will fill—a "suitable helper," one who will complete Adam and reign with him in their calling to tend the garden.

AMP (Gen. 3:1)

Now the serpent was more subtle and crafty than any living creature of the field that the Lord God had made. And he [Satan] said to the woman, Can it really be that God has said, You shall not eat from every tree of the garden?

WEJ-Paraphrase (Gen. 3:1)

The devil leverages and exploits the characteristics of the serpent and communicates his deception effectively through innuendos: God is withholding good things from you, so God must not be trustworthy or kind; Adam may have misheard God's direction; God does not have the authority to make special rules for humanity. The devil targets Eve because she is the completion and helpmate to Adam. However, she is built to fight alongside Adam, rather than solo. Satan knows that if he can take down Eve, then he can likely take down Adam.

- *Where is Adam's involvement? Where is Eve's concern that Adam's involvement is missing?*

AMP (Gen. 3:2)

In addition, the woman said to the serpent, We may eat the fruit from the trees of the garden

WEJ-Paraphrase (Gen. 3:2)

Eve is unalarmed by this conversation because she doesn't understand the specifics of what God stated. She paraphrases God's words, putting the emphasis in the wrong places. She gets "eat" right but forgets "freely" and "every." Just like Satan, she restated the command from her own vantage point, not trusting God's command the way it was given.

- *Where is Adam's involvement? Where is Eve's concern that Adam's involvement is missing?*

To go deeper on section 4.1,
Visit www.ThePowerOfAHoneymoon.com/phmtools

Writing Activity 4.2:

- 4.2.1. After reviewing the disharmony and fall Adam and Eve experienced in their relationship, are there practical benefits this story can offer for your marriage or your future marriage? Alternatively, for the single, male or female, what blazing clarity does this passage bring to your daily life?

_____
_____

- 4.2.2. From your reading, why do Adam and Eve have different responsibilities and, thus, accountability?

_____
_____

- 4.2.3. Did you realize that God gave Adam a command about tending the garden that Eve was not there to hear?

_____
_____

- 4.2.4. How might the husband and the wife, or the single hold securely from distortion, a mandate that God communicates to them?

_____
_____

Positive Takeaways from the First-Ever Unsuccessful Marriage

The most revolutionary thing that happened to me on my honeymoon night was my understanding of my role to cover, protect, and care for my beloved bride. This message was sent from heaven directly to my spirit. I felt enormous clarity about this new purpose that I was commissioned for. First, I was to find the target—God's plan and purpose for our marriage—then I was to build a safeguard around it. How do you build a safeguard around your marriage? Alternatively, as a single, how do you build a safeguard around your married life with Christ, and your daily life? That is discussed in the next chapter.

Similarly, my beloved bride relished her new life mission: to receive the protection and nurture of her groom. Securing our new callings as husband and wife was fun and rewarding. We quickly found that we could thrive in our roles with the spiritual allotment we received from God's word and God's Spirit.

For multimedia companion on this section #4.3.1,
Visit www.ThePowerOfAHoneymoon.com/phmmedia

Your "What Choices to Get Right Always" By the Authentic Blueprint Activities

Reading Activity 4.3: Genesis 3:1 – 3:19

Now read the story surrounding the marriage failure, Genesis 3:1 – 3:19. Then, look at some key passages with me below and consider them in their original context, emphasis and timeless impact.

AMP (Gen. 3:6)

> Moreover, when the woman saw that the tree was good (suitable, pleasant) for food and that it was delightful to look at, and a tree to be desired in order to make one wise, she took of its fruit and ate; and she gave some also to her husband, and he ate.

WEJ-Paraphrase (Gen. 3:6)

> The enemy invited Eve into a trap with his conversation, and the trap was possible to be escaped. Unfortunately, Eve chose to exercise overly independent actions apart from God and Adam that led her into perils. Adam chose passive and negligent leadership as shown in how he was not involved in the conversation; he had not refuted and obliterated falsity about God and God's plush

purpose for his and Eve's marriage. Despite being the perfectly joined first couple, their negligence in the design of marriage was the cause of their downfall.

The serpent set a trap that was possible to escape. Satan attempted the identical tactic of questioning God's instruction to Jesus, but Jesus confronted him correctly and undid the serpent's traps. (The story is told in Matthew 4:1-11.)

Adam and Eve resorted to convenience. It was more convenient for Adam to do what Eve said to do than, rather than to exert his energy in staying vigilant in his role to protect, lead, and obey God. Eve attempted outwitting the serpent's challenge based on her ingenuity and strength. She should have crushed the lies of the enemy or told God or Adam about the conversation with the serpent. Instead, she chose not to, and she fell for Satan's lies.

AMP (Gen. 3:7)

Then the eyes of them both were opened, and they knew that they were naked; and they sewed fig leaves together and made themselves aprons like girdles.

WEJ-Paraphrase (Gen. 3:7)

A sudden break occurs in the closeness and intimacy Adam and Eve had experienced with each other and with God. Contrast this verse with Genesis 2:25: "And the man and his wife were both naked and were not embarrassed or ashamed in each other's presence."

AMP (Gen. 3:8-9)

⁸ And they heard the sound of the Lord God walking in the garden in the cool of the day, and Adam and his wife hid themselves from the presence of the Lord God among the trees of the garden. ⁹ But the Lord God called to Adam and said to him, Where are you?

WEJ-Paraphrase (Gen. 3:8-9)

Father Lord, with perfect knowledge *intimates I know you are hiding because of a guilty conscience from disobedience and your shame of sin, and fear of impending consequence. But if I do not seek you out, your coping mechanism will continue to go inward and cause an implosion. Instead, I want you to stop trying to fix the problem wrongly, such as hiding away from me. Instead, I want you to come get in dialogue with me.*

- **Honeymoon Living Key:** God always chooses relationship with us! He is not scared of our sin. Instead, he invites us to choose running to Him in our weakness instead of hiding from Him.

AMP (Gen. 3:10)

He said, I heard the sound of You [walking] in the garden, and I was afraid because I was naked; and I hid myself.

WEJ-Paraphrase (Gen. 3:10)

Adam is saying *I was hiding because I did not want to see you in my shame and guilty condition. Instead, I was hoping to hide for as long as possible, just to not take ownership that I failed you. And I don't yet have remorse for my failings, and hence I will halt or delay my healing and fixing the problem.*

AMP (Gen. 3:11)

And He said, Who told you that you were naked? Have you eaten of the tree of which I commanded you that you should not eat?

WEJ-Paraphrase (Gen. 3:11)

Father Lord invites Adam a second time to see the problem he started since Adam does not admit: *I have sinned and have shame by the act and error of disobeying You, The Lord and Father. I am fearful of what my punishment will be. But I prefer to forgo giving You my embarrassment. Although it begins the process of taking away the barrier of my shame between You and I. This shame is also now is between Eve and I, but I am not willing to correct the failing I have, nor to throw myself on the mercy and grace of my loving Father, and the Lord.*

AMP (Gen. 3:12)

And the man said, The woman whom You gave to be with me—she gave me [fruit] from the tree, and I ate.

WEJ-Paraphrase (Gen. 3:12)

Father Lord's appeal to Adam was not just a question, but the invitation and opportunity to stop further hiding and running away. Adam's response is instead psychologically to deflect the Lord's offer. Adam refuses to admit his disobedience and sin and chooses the excuse: *Eve is the reason and cause to my disobeying the Lord.* Indirectly he is saying, *The Lord maybe could have been at fault because He gave him the circumstance of a woman helpmate.*

AMP (Gen. 3:13)

And the Lord God said to the woman, What is this you have done? And the woman said, The serpent beguiled (cheated, outwitted, and deceived) me, and I ate.

WEJ-Paraphrase (Gen. 3:13)

Father Lord invites Eve not to pretend everything is okay, and their disobedience was not a minor infraction. She professes, *she was outwitted but implies she did nothing wrong of her own.*

4 THE FIRST "FAILED" MARRIAGE

AMP (Gen. 3:17)

And to Adam He said, Because you have listened and given heed to the voice of your wife and have eaten of the tree of which I commanded you, saying, You shall not eat of it, the ground is under a curse because of you; in sorrow and toil shall you eat [of the fruits] of it all the days of your life.

WEJ-Paraphrase (Gen. 3:17)

Father Lord reveals the negative consequences that Adam brought on himself. Adam, *your excuse and blaming Eve does not show remorse and acknowledgement that you were clearly to lead, and protect, and steward all I entrusted to you, with to be your companion for this one thing. You did know better. And you are at fault, the ground you would have ruled with ease can no longer let you rule it or submit to you for your lack of submission to the Lord, its maker.*

Writing Activity 4.4:

- 4.4.1. Did the fall have to happen? Why, or why not?

_____

_____

- 4.4.2. What wrong choices did Eve and Adam make?

_____

_____

- 4.4.3. Did you see the enemy being strategic in approaching Eve versus Adam? Why, or why not?

_____

_____

- 4.4.4. Did you see Adam and Eve not being vigilant on each other's behalf? How might this bring clarity to the husband and wife, as they guard against intrusion in their marriage and fulfill the calling on their marriage? Alternatively, for the single, male or female, what blazing clarity does this passage bring to your daily life?

_____

_____

To go deeper on section 4.4,
   Visit www.*ThePowerOfAHoneymoon.com/phmtools*

✻ ✻ ✻

Blueprint Four Summary

A summary of Blueprint IV is found in Genesis 2:15; 3:1.

Our exquisite purpose and bountiful blessings <u>must be guarded</u> against the common enemy to God.

Part 1 of 3, God built Adam and Eve with a purpose to fulfill and gifts to steward. In His guidance, Adam and Eve had a built-in safeguard if they stayed actively living under God's guidance and to His purpose. God guided Adam and Eve to **eat freely of every tree except one,** *and this would ensure there was no separation in the relationship between them and God. (Gen. 2:15, 16-17; 1:28)*

Part 2 of 3, God built Adam and Eve to possess uniquely crafted and suitable roles for each other that together made the two a complete unassailable whole. God didn't make Adam and Eve to function as two undifferentiated individuals, with indistinguishable leadership duties. (Gen. 2:7, 15; 3:8–9, 11)

Part 3 of 3, The one enemy of God can only suggest lies. No matter what lie the enemy suggests, whether it be about God, His created purpose for us, or His care for us, God's guidance comes with a strategy and safety to withstand the enemy's lies. If we don't rely on God's guidance, then a similar consequence to that which Adam and Eve experienced will ensue, e.g., a fractured relationship with God, spiritual distance, and disunity within a marriage, living with or in **shame, and hiding from God.** *(Gen. 3:1; 2:7, 25; 3:8)*

4 THE FIRST "FAILED" MARRIAGE

Sometimes a picture or diagram can communicate a thousand words.
The diagram below is the Genesis story, which captures the first relationship failure (Adam and Eve falling out of relationship with God), and the fall of the first marriage.

Legend to the diagram:
1) In the beginning, God created Adam and Eve to carry out a purpose.
2) The line that comes from the enemy symbolizes one lie after another. (Satan has the nickname of "Father of Lies.")
3) Adam or Eve didn't stay focused on living out the truth God gave them.

Synopsis of the diagram:
The enemy doesn't have power but can only suggest lies.
These lies aren't worth us investing our time in to finding out what is enlightening about them. They are lies from a master of lies, and hence God desires us to forgo debating with the enemy about the lies. Also, the lies the enemy speaks to us can never produce understanding; rather they are his means to attempt to plant deception or contaminate trust in God.
Additionally, the lies are meant to distract from staying focused on our purpose for living. Lastly, the enemy uses his lies to try to trick us to misuse our gifts and the blessings God has given us.
The individual or couple who does not live in submission and fellowship with God through a dependent relationship with Jesus will not find Jesus' steady protective armor. Nor will their life's purpose (and, when married, their married purpose) be unstoppable against any antics of the enemy.

The Genesis Story Diagramed

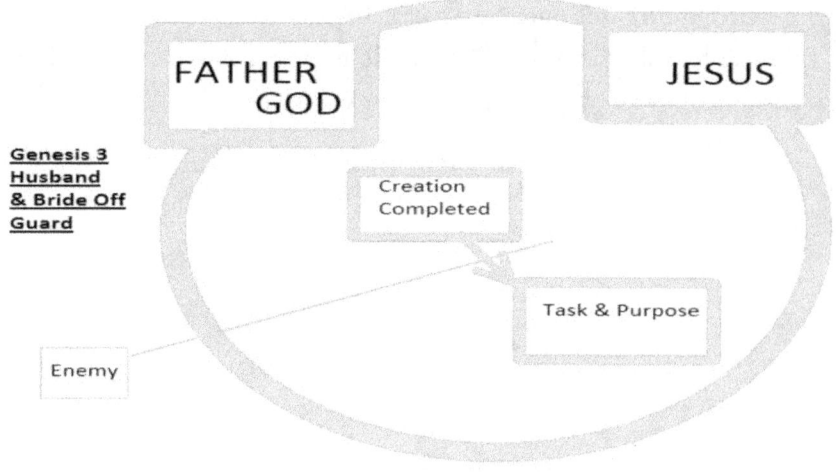

Keeping Marriage War-Zone Free

When my bride and I had learned the passages in this chapter (during our dating), we discovered the importance of being allies in our roles as husband and wife. Staying in close unity ensures we are impenetrable to temptation and able to present one another as holy before God, who holds us accountable for the way we steward our talents, our future children, and the earth. In addition, the enemy of God (though already defeated) seeks to entrap and derail couples, so they will be ineffective in fulfilling God's work in their lives and marriage. We are committed to giving the devil no space to thrive in our marriage relationship.

Genesis 2 and 3 show how quickly chaos will ensue in marriage and how quickly the closeness and oneness of Adam and Eve degraded to hiding from each other and being separated from each other rather than united as one. In addition, these passages show the value of the husband and wife roles built into God's design of the marriage union. The enemy came strategically to target Eve, and it was consequential that the catastrophic marriage union failure happened at the same time Adam did not show his leadership or act out to resist, protect, or even to die in the act of protecting God's mandate to steward the garden explicitly given to Adam. Adam acting out in his lead role, and Eve collaborating with Adam, and/or God would have been the key to withstanding the enemy's attacks.

This chapter told the story of how to do marriage the wrong way, but the next chapter shows how to do it the right way. Let's go

5 THE FIRST FAILED MARRIAGE "REWRITTEN"

In this chapter, we will cover part three of the authentic marriage blueprint, when Jesus restored God's original marriage design and defeated the enemy to make vibrant marriages a reality again.

Just a Quick Review of Our Three Previous Chapters

A $900 million incident showed us that we might have a crisis in our understanding of marriage. If we have any crack in our understanding of marriage, it would be a no-brainer to take the $900 million and walk away from our marriages. Whether boldly or sheepishly, we would likely take the offer if we have any disconnect with God's authentic marriage blueprint.

However, if we know that "bone of my bone and flesh of my flesh" is God's reality—not some over-the-top poetics from a fairy tale starring Adam and Eve—this will give us encouragement to walk away from the money and back to our spouse. What a humongous mess it would be to untwine two spouses from each other after God has supernaturally joined them together? Divorce was clearly never part of God's intent in the original marriage blueprint. No manner of sophisticated divorce arrangements can separate what God has joined together in Adam and Eve and in every married couple after them. At best, it would be like a botched surgery to attempt to separate two people united in marriage.

Adding fuel to the fire, every marriage has a common problem: the anti-partner, the enemy of God. This is the same enemy Adam and Eve faced, and he persists as the enemy of every married person (and every future married person). Facing his attacks is the reality of life on earth, until the final judgment day when God will put the already-defeated devil in hell for good. Since marriage is a powerful and integral part of God's agenda (covered in Chapter 12), the enemy cannot stand to see your marriage properly built and sustainably fueled by God.

Is There a "Real" Successful Husband?

Jesus actually defeated this enemy at the cross. Jesus defeated him on two levels concerning marriage. First, Jesus offers us an example of how to do marriage right after our misdirection from Adam and Eve. Second, with the premium grade nuclear fuel of agape love unleashed by Jesus after the resurrection and passed on to us through by the Holy Spirit, we spouses (and future spouses) now have access to a fresh and daily dose of it to power our marriages.

We can be joined intricately and spiritually with our spouses through the Holy Spirit and His agape love. We can love our spouses extravagantly, and together we can rampage enemy territory through our joint gifts.

Interjecting a brief moment of gratitude and thanksgiving: Thank you God for Jesus, the solution to our marriages, and Your Holy Spirit, the conduit of your agape love (covered more fully in the next chapter).

Your "What is a Real Husband" By the Authentic Blueprint Activities
ACTIVITY INSTRUCTIONS

The rest of this chapter is in an interactive workbook format.

How? We will frequently prompt the readers to pause and observe, answer questions, brainstorm, or invite them to check out external tools to get further help. Also note: when an activity references scripture passages, we encourage you to follow along in The Scriptures, using your Bible or one online. In most activities, we will use The Amplified® Bible Translation,

(AMP). Then we will make a summary observation of the scripture passage verse by verse, which will be labeled "WEJ-Paraphrase."

Why? FIRST, so you the reader can gain the maximum benefit through participation. **SECOND,** to permit later interactive activities to be-added-on, and accelerate the benefits you gain from the material. **THIRD,** to permit a bridge to have later live interaction with authors and teams dedicated to championing your success in singlehood, marriage, and love by God's design. **FORTH,** as you work through the activities below, you may find yourself wanting to go deeper and explore more.

Additional tools and support at:
www.ThePowerOfAHoneymoon.com/phmtools

Reading Activity 5.1: Ephesians 5:25–5:29

Read how Jesus (the second Adam) rewrote the role of the husband and restored the design of marriage in Ephesians 5:25–5:29. Then, look at some key passages with me below and consider their timeless impact on the rewritten husband role in marriage.

AMP (Eph. 5:25)

> Husbands, love your wives, as Christ loved the church and gave Himself up for her

WEJ-Paraphrase (Eph. 5:25)

In marriage, spouses enter into a supernatural triune relationship between themselves and the Lord.

The husband has a mandate to supernaturally and utterly prioritize the Lord's will first, just as Christ prioritized the Lord's will and selflessly obeyed God the Father (even to His crucifixion). Also, husbands are to follow the example of Christ's love for the church and love their wives selflessly and unconditionally.

AMP (Eph. 5:26)

So that He might sanctify her, having cleansed her by the washing of water with the Word

WEJ-Paraphrase (Eph. 5:26)

Continuing with Christ as the model, husbands are to love their brides wholly and to encourage them toward holiness just as Christ loves the church, His Bride, and leads her toward wholeness through His life-giving actions and words.

AMP (Eph. 5:27)

That He might present the church to Himself in glorious splendor, without spot or wrinkle or any such things [that she might be holy and faultless].

WEJ-Paraphrase (Eph. 5:27)

Husbands have a tall order to fulfill in emulating Christ's love for His church. No husband will have ever "arrived" in fulfilling his divine duties to his wife with Christ as his model.

Christ formed a "people" out of those who were formerly not a people (the body), and Christ joined himself to those people, His Bride the church, so that they might become perfect and spotless through His love. Therefore, husbands ought to pass along to their brides what they have received from Christ the Lord.

AMP (Eph. 5:28)

Even so, husbands should love their wives as [being in a sense] their own bodies. He who loves his own wife loves himself.

WEJ-Paraphrase (Eph. 5:28)

Husbands must realize the reality of their oneness with their own wife is as literal as the oneness that Adam and Eve shared. The wife is not an appendage, an add-on, or a negligible bonus attachment to him.

The husband and wife are interwoven parts of an intricate engine. **The husband (using agape love)** lubricates the engine to stave off the damaging friction between the two that could ultimately impair them reaching their calling. He and his wife have a real mandate from God to arrive at their destination using their fuel optimally.

Therefore, it is not hyperbole to say that a husband who loves his wife well is actually caring for his own body well. Likewise, a husband cannot truly love (or care for) himself while neglecting his wife.

AMP (Eph. 5:29)

For no man ever hated his own flesh, but nourishes and carefully protects and cherishes it, as Christ does the church

WEJ-Paraphrase (Eph. 5:29)

The total all-encompassing love Christ has for the church body ought to be the same type of total love the husband has for his wife, because in marriage, the wife is part of the husband's body.

Also, just as Christ provides spiritual nourishment, covering, and affection to the church through His Word and His Holy Spirit, so the husband should nourish, protect, and cherish his wife.

To go deeper on section 5.1,
Visit www.ThePowerOfAHoneymoon.com/phmtools

Writing Activity 5.2:

- 5.2.1. After reviewing Jesus' demonstration of the marriage standard God has for the husband, are there practical benefits this passage can offer the husband in your marriage or your future marriage? Alternatively, for the single, male or female, what blazing clarity does this passage bring to your daily life?

_____
_____

- 5.2.2. From your reading, how is Jesus primarily a model for husbands rather than wives?

_____
_____

- 5.2.3. Is the example of Jesus supposed to be just poetic? Or should it provide daily guidance to husbands?

_____
_____

- 5.2.4. How might this clarity for the husband help him empower his bride?

_____
_____

Is There a "Real" Successful Wife?

Although the beauty of the Garden of Eden would have been an enormous gift to Adam and Eve, the greater gift was having unhindered access to God, their Father and Creator. Likewise, while on earth, Christ-followers have similar access to the Father through Christ, and the Holy Spirit. However, the ultimate access and fellowship with God will be in full effect at the wedding between Christ and His Bride the Church.

Being a bride is big deal in earthly terms, even in the modern culture and throughout history. *The wedding day is "her day," she is the most ornately dressed and is the most beautiful in the room. The wedding starts when the bride walks down the aisle, and everybody stands in her honor.* Being a bride is even a bigger deal in heavenly terms. The Scriptures portray the culminating celebration of the Church as the Bride of Christ in captivating terms. The Bride is beautifully ornate and has a magnificent entry in the ultimate wedding and marriage. The following scripture passage is an example of Christ's Bride's glorious portrayal.

> *² And I saw the holy city, the new Jerusalem, descending out of heaven from God, all arrayed like a bride beautified and adorned for her husband; ³ Then I heard a mighty voice from the throne and I perceived its distinct words, saying, See! The abode of God is with men, and He will live (encamp, tent) among them; and they shall be His people, and God shall personally be with them and be their God. (Revelation 21:2-3, AMP)*

The ultimate destination of the Church as the Bride of Christ speaks of the worth Christ places in the Bride. In the meantime, before the heavenly realization of the wedding feast, Scripture conveys practical guidance for the Christian wife from the imagery of the spiritual Bride of Christ. What is Scriptures' tangible guidance on being a successful bride on earth?

For multimedia companion on this section #5.3.1,

Visit www.ThePowerOfAHoneymoon.com/phmmedia

Your "What is a Real Wife" By the Authentic Blueprint Activities

Reading Activity 5.3: Ephesians 5:22–5:24

Read how the Christian church as The Bride of Christ rewrote the role of a wife and restored God's original intention of marriage in Ephesians 5:22–5:24. Then, look at some key passages with me below and consider their timeless impact on the rewritten wife role in marriage.

AMP (Eph. 5:22)

Wives, be subject (be submissive and adapt yourselves) to your own husbands as [a service] to the Lord.

WEJ-Paraphrase (Eph. 5:22)

The Lord continues His original plan for humanity by showing us the way back to Eden. His intentions at creation are still intact and attainable through scriptural guidance. To join her husband as one flesh and to leave all others while cleaving to her husband, the wife must embrace God's plan for the oneness between a husband and wife. The Christian wife must treat her husband as her spiritual protector and warrior. The respect she once gave to her parents before marriage should now be given to her husband. And the relationship she once had with the Lord on her own is now channeled through her love and service to her husband. This is not saying she must go to her husband to talk to God. It is saying she cannot partition her spiritual leading patterns to be as if she was single and not joined to her husband.

AMP (Eph. 5:23)

For the husband is head of the wife as Christ is the Head of the church, Himself the Savior of [His] body.

WEJ-Paraphrase (Eph. 5:23)

The reason Christian wives should submit to their husbands is because the church, which is the body of Christ and a model for wives, submits to Christ, the head. Just as Christ is over the church, so too the husband, as head of the marriage, is over the wife. Meaning, the husband must double and triple down on his spiritual depth so that he can get more than enough of God's wisdom and guidance, not just for himself, but more than enough to nourish his bride ultimately to God's ideal for her. Therefore, the husband will be submitting to God and getting fresh guidance for God for them both.

5 THE FIRST FAILED MARRIAGE "REWRITTEN"

AMP (Eph. 5:24)

As the church is subject to Christ, so let wives also be subject in everything to their husbands.

WEJ-Paraphrase (Eph. 5:24)

The church comes before Christ with a willing, trusting, and loving subordination, and likewise the wife lovingly submits first to the Lord and then to the spiritual will of her husband.

AMP (Eph. 5:21)

Be subject to one another out of reverence for Christ (the Messiah, the Anointed One).

WEJ-Paraphrase (Eph. 5:21)

(I intentionally address verse 21 out of sequence)

It functions well as a disclaimer to the above passages on submission, the Christian husband, the Christian Wife, and the Christian Single will fail by using their ingenuity, self-will or pass experience with God to succeed in a current vibrant and fresh relationship with God or their spouse. Instead, the ability to submit spiritually to God or in a marital union comes from a loving and trusting relationship with God through Jesus. It is important to understand the above biblical command to spiritual submission to be impossible if done in human strength, and then the solution can be blindingly clear. Essential to succeed in God's design for marriage or singlehood is a current active relationship with God through prayer, scripture reading, cultivating talent for The Lord and living by the Holy Spirit's guidance. The dependency dynamic between a husband and wife, or a single person and God is the same dependency dynamic that originated when Adam was breathed into by God to be made alive. Spiritual submission is similar to agreeing with God about the dependency dynamic that each human is in with God. As we submit to God, we keep tuned up in our spiritual wiring back to God. The process of submitting consumes the fuel of the Holy Spirit, hence our frequent reliance on The Lord and the needed relationship with Him and the Holy Spirit.

To go deeper on section 5.3,
Visit www.T*hePowerOfAHoneymoon.com/phmtools*

Writing Activity 5.4:

- 5.4.1. After reviewing how the church demonstrates God's standard of marriage for wives, what practical benefits can this story offer for the wife of your marriage or future marriage? Alternatively, for the single, male or female, what blazing clarity does this passage bring to your daily life?

  _____
  _____

- 5.4.2. From your reading, why is the church a model for wives rather than husbands?

  _____
  _____

- 5.4.3. Is the example of the church as Christ's Bride supposed to be just poetic? Or should it provide daily guidance to wives?

  _____
  _____

- 5.4.4. How might this clarity for the wife help her support the husband in his purposes?

  _____
  _____

To go deeper on section 5.4,
Visit www.T*hePowerOfAHoneymoon.com/phmtools*

5 THE FIRST FAILED MARRIAGE "REWRITTEN"

Sometimes a picture or diagram can communicate a thousand words. The diagram below is the Genesis story infused with the New Testament Story of Christ coming as the solution to the first relationship problem. His solution applies to problems found when a person is single or married.

Legend to the diagram:
1) Whether single or married, Christ intervenes as a practical role model to offer rewritten guidance on effectively relating to God and fulfilling our life purpose. For the married, Christ shows us the way to make our marriage thrive. **2)** Jesus is an impenetrable armor. **3)** The enemy is as powerless to thwart a couple or a person in singlehood as Satan was powerless to thwart Jesus when Jesus came on earth to do the Father's will. Jesus didn't let Satan's lie penetrate him.

Synopsis of the diagram:
Christ is our ultimate protector. He provides the singularly effective weapon to His followers to stay victorious against the enemy's attacks. Specifically, Christ provides the truth and Holy Spirit-empowered strength to keep our daily paths straight despite the lies the enemy disseminates in an attempt to distract, confuse, or mislead us. Because Christ corrected the relationship that went awry when Adam and Eve sinned, now the single or married can keep focused on fulfilling their life purpose. Marriage can be the bliss and boon that God means for it. Alternatively, for the single, he or she can daily thrive in their season of singlehood. The individual or couple who lives in submission and fellowship with God through a dependent relationship with Jesus will find that Jesus' protective armor is impenetrable and will firmly keep one unstoppable in their life purpose, despite any antics of the enemy.

The Ephesians Story Diagramed

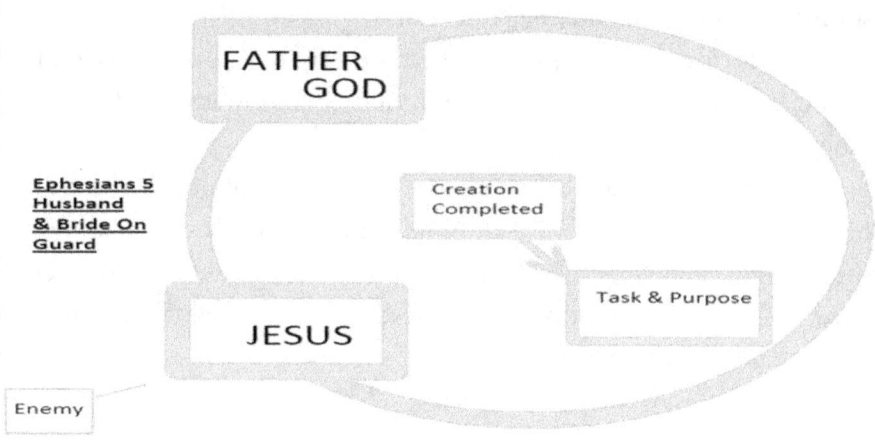

Blueprint Five Summary

A summary of Blueprint V is found in Ephesians 5:25–29.

Our original exquisite purpose and bountiful blessings have been restored by the demonstration of Jesus' relationship with God and the Church, the bride of Christ.

Part 1 of 3, Jesus as the obedient son of God replaces the example of the children of God relationship set by Adam and Eve. (The Four Gospels and Romans 8:14–17)

Part 2 of 3, Jesus as the husband to the Church replaces the example of the husband set by Adam. (Eph. 5:25–29 and The Four Gospels)

Part 3 of 3, The Church as the Bride of Christ replaces example of the wife set by Eve. (Eph. 5:22–24 and The Four Gospels)

Keeping Marriage Simple

When my bride and I had learned the passages in this chapter (during our dating), we discovered the jackpot. We will succeed in marriage because the scales tip in our favor through Christ and the Holy Spirit.

There are two significant takeaways. The husband should always seek to achieve God's standard as a spiritual leader, not the standard set by his own father or other men he knows. Happily aiming toward Christ's standard of spiritual leadership makes my path clear.

Similarly, my bride walks with blazing clarity toward a marriage that is secure and capable of great things for God because we have His amazing blueprint to follow.

This chapter focused on Ephesians 5 and The Scripture's teaching about how to do marriage right. In addition, we talked about the good news of the defeated enemy of God and how the Christian will be a victor over the enemy in his or her marriage. In the next chapter, we will talk about God's amazing love and rewarding finish line!

6 WHAT IS A HONEYMOON REALLY SUPPOSED TO BE?

In this chapter, we will cover part four of the authentic marriage blueprint, when God the Father gets the last word on the quality of love we are called to have. Since Ephesians showed us that Jesus and the church are our examples for marriage, by studying the life of Jesus in Scriptures and living through the Holy Spirit, we can attain the bliss of marriage. We have every advantage stacked in our favor for our marriages to succeed. We must just show up, rely on the Holy Spirit for renewal, and pour out the love God provides us with each day. What a plan for loving our spouses (or future spouses) radically (living like you are still on your honeymoon with the love of your life, looking and behaving love-smitten, or for the not-yet-married, living a pure and fulfilled single life, empowered by the Spirit)!

Part four sums up God's desire that we live out *daily* His agape love, not just on our honeymoon (or during anniversaries, special occasions, etc.), but all the time. But how is this possible?

Is There a "Real" Definition of "Love"?

The formal definition of love from God's vantage point is found in 1 Corinthians 13. When you receive God's report card about how you are doing with loving others, you learn a few things about how He thinks about love. God does not idly set standards without calling us to meet them. Let's jump into 1 Corinthians 13 to find God's blueprint for love.

Your "What is Love" By the Authentic Blueprint Activities
ACTIVITY INSTRUCTIONS

The rest of this chapter is in an interactive workbook format.

How? We will frequently prompt the readers to pause and observe, answer questions, brainstorm, or invite them to check out external tools to get further help. *Also note: when an activity references scripture passages, we encourage you to follow along in The Scriptures, using your Bible or one online. In most activities, we will use The Amplified® Bible Translation, (AMP). Then we will make a summary observation of the scripture passage verse by verse, which will be labeled "WEJ-Paraphrase."*

Why? FIRST, so you the reader can gain the maximum benefit through participation. **SECOND**, to permit later interactive activities to be-added-on, and accelerate the benefits you gain from the material. **THIRD**, to permit a bridge to have later live interaction with authors and teams dedicated to championing your success in singlehood, marriage, and love by God's design. **FORTH**, as you work through the activities below, you may find yourself wanting to go deeper and explore more.

Additional tools and support at:
www.ThePowerOfAHoneymoon.com/phmtools

Reading Activity 6.1: 1 Corinthians 13

Read about the real love that fuels God-honoring relationships, including the marriage relationship, in 1 Corinthians 13. Then, look at some key passages with me below and consider their practical impact on marriage.

I found a trick to reading 1 Corinthians 13. It makes the most sense to me when I reorder the verses in this fashion: v7, v1-6, v13, v11-12, v9-10, and v7-8. Here is my wrestling with and paraphrasing of it in that order.

AMP (1 Cor. 13:7)

> Love bears up under anything and everything that comes, is ever ready to believe the best of every person, its hopes are fadeless under all circumstances, and it endures everything [without weakening].

6 WHAT IS A HONEYMOON REALLY SUPPOSED TO BE?

WEJ-Paraphrase (1 Cor. 13:7)

Here in 1 Corinthians 13 is a detailed description of what real love is, real agape love. There is no substitute for agape love—none.

AMP (1 Cor. 13:1)

If I [can] speak in the tongues of men and [even] of angels, but have not love (that reasoning, intentional, spiritual devotion such as is inspired by God's love for and in us), I am only a noisy gong or a clanging cymbal.

WEJ-Paraphrase (1 Cor. 13:1)

Agape love is more than just wonderful oration or motivational pep talks.

AMP (1 Cor. 13:2)

In addition, if I have prophetic powers (the gift of interpreting the divine will and purpose), and understand all the secret truths and mysteries and possess all knowledge, and if I have [sufficient] faith so that I can remove mountains, but have not love (God's love in me) I am nothing (a useless nobody).

WEJ-Paraphrase (1 Cor. 13:2)

Agape love does more than casts a vision. Demonstrating tangible results or material productivity is no substitute for agape love.

AMP (1 Cor. 13:3)

Even if I dole out all that I have [to the poor in providing] food, and if I surrender my body to be burned or in order that I may glory, but have not love (God's love in me), I gain nothing.

WEJ-Paraphrase (1 Cor. 13:3)

Nor will outstanding altruism and alms giving and other self-sacrificial acts substitute for agape love.

AMP (1 Cor. 13:4)

Love endures long and is patient and kind; love never is envious nor boils over with jealousy, is not boastful or vainglorious, and does not display itself haughtily.

WEJ-Paraphrase (1 Cor. 13:4)

Only if your utter and singular motivation for your actions is agape love will you remain steadfast, especially if the people you love are acting unkind or distancing themselves from you.

AMP (1 Cor. 13:5)

It is not conceited (arrogant and inflated with pride); it is not rude (unmannerly) and does not act unbecomingly. Love (God's love in us) does not insist on its own rights or its own way, for it is not self-seeking; it is not touchy or fretful or resentful; it takes no account of the evil done to it [it pays no attention to a suffered wrong].

WEJ-Paraphrase (1 Cor. 13:5)

Actions performed out of anything but agape love will not last and will be tainted by human feelings (like pride, rudeness, fear, revenge, etcetera).

AMP (1 Cor. 13:6)

It does not rejoice at injustice and unrighteousness, but rejoices when right and truth prevail.

WEJ-Paraphrase (1 Cor. 13:6)

Agape love cannot be confused with actions that cut corners for the sake of convenience or accommodation or take advantage of others through clever negotiations or one-sided compromises.

6 WHAT IS A HONEYMOON REALLY SUPPOSED TO BE?

AMP (1 Cor. 13:13)

And so faith, hope, love abide [faith—conviction and belief respecting man's relation to God and divine things; hope—joyful and confident expectation of eternal salvation; love—true affection for God and man, growing out of God's love for and in us], these three; but the greatest of these is love.

WEJ-Paraphrase (1 Cor. 13:13)

Agape love brings heaven to earth—infinite, perfect, universal, divine heavenly love brought down into the finite world.

AMP (1 Cor. 13:11)

When I was a child, I talked like a child, I thought like a child, I reasoned like a child; now that I have become a man, I am done with childish ways and have put them aside.

WEJ-Paraphrase (1 Cor. 13:11)

If you want to grow up and truly fulfill God's call for you, love radically with agape love and set aside selfishness and immaturity.

AMP (1 Cor. 13:12)

For now we are looking in a mirror that gives only a dim (blurred) reflection [of reality as in a riddle or enigma], but then [when perfection comes] we shall see in reality and face to face! Now I know in part (imperfectly), but then I shall know and understand fully and clearly, even in the same manner as I have been fully and clearly known and understood [by God].

WEJ-Paraphrase (1 Cor. 13:12)

Otherwise, much of your day-to-day life will be jagged and disjointed.

AMP (1 Cor. 13:9)

For our knowledge is fragmentary (incomplete and imperfect), and our prophecy (our teaching) is fragmentary (incomplete and imperfect).

WEJ-Paraphrase (1 Cor. 13:9)

For this is just the nature of things, since no knowledge or inspiration is or was meant to be the end goal.

AMP (1 Cor. 13:10)

But when the complete and perfect (total) comes, the incomplete and imperfect will vanish away (become antiquated, void, and superseded).

WEJ-Paraphrase (1 Cor. 13:10)

They are just a means to the end goal of agape love.

AMP (1 Cor. 13:7)

Love bears up under anything and everything that comes, is ever ready to believe the best of every person, its hopes are fadeless under all circumstances, and it endures everything [without weakening].

WEJ-Paraphrase (1 Cor. 13:7)

Here is a recap: let your motivation (or fuel for each action) be God's agape love. Be long-suffering, trust in the gift of God, and share it with someone else. You are called to the long-term purpose and calling of loving others, whatever hard work may be needed along the way to see it come to fruition.

AMP (1 Cor. 13:8)

Love never fails [never fades out or becomes obsolete or comes to an end]. As for prophecy (the gift of interpreting the divine will and purpose), it will be fulfilled and pass away; as for tongues, they will be destroyed and cease; as for knowledge, it will pass away [it will lose its value and be superseded by truth].

WEJ-Paraphrase (1 Cor. 13:8)

There is no substitute to love for fueling all that is miraculous in yours or other people's lives. Wisdom and useful facts and figures are no substitute for love when it comes to transforming you or the person you are called to love.

To go deeper on section 6.1,
Visit www.ThePowerOfAHoneymoon.com/phmtools

Writing Activity 6.2:

- 6.2.1. After reviewing the standard God has for love is agape love for all relationships, especially the marriage relationship, what are the practical benefits this chapter offers to your marriage or your future marriage?

_____
_____

- 6.2.2. When do you feel most loving toward others?

_____

- 6.2.3. Is it before or after you have been in the presence of God?

Before_____ / After_____

- 6.2.4. Is it before or after you have been in prayer for that person?

Before_____ / After_____

- 6.2.5. Is it when you maintain a childlike faith and sincerity toward God and His calling and His provision for you?

Yes____ / No____

To go deeper on section 6.2,
    Visit www.ThePowerOfAHoneymoon.com/phmtools

What Makes Love "For Real"?

A honeymoon marriage is a marriage powered by your first love for God. Honeymoon living is a series of choices to stay on the straight and narrow path of cherishing each other by first and ever-increasingly cherishing God. We grow in our love for God by deepening our knowledge of Him through his word and by responding in obedience through loving actions toward God and others. As we grow more in love with God, he helps us to grow in our roles as husband and wife. We can put away childish games and rules in our marriage relationships. There is no other formula for a successful marriage than to love God with all your heart, mind, soul, and strength, and to love your spouse as you love yourself through these same four categories: heart, soul, mind and strength. Loving your spouse less than 100 percent in any one of these four categories will not do.

During our honeymoon in Cancun, Elyssa and I both were aiming for 100 percent in these four categories (heart, mind, soul, and strength). But it went beyond the honeymoon. From the moment we entered into our marriage union, we committed to loving each other this way from then on and in increasing measure. We had no plans to see how little love we could get by with before our marriage suffered. We wanted God's best the whole way.

First-love living is what God requires of us for loving Himself.

For multimedia companion on this section #6.2.5,
    Visit www.ThePowerOfAHoneymoon.com/phmmedia

Your "How Does it All Turn Out" Activities

Reading Activity 6.3: Revelations 2

Read about the first-love gold standard by which God the Father judges everything, including marriage and dating relationships for spouses and singles, found in Revelations 2:1-7. Then, look at some key passages with me below and consider their practical impact on marriage:

AMP (Rev. 2:1)

> To the angel (messenger) of the assembly (church) in Ephesus write: These are the words of Him Who holds the seven stars [which are the messengers of the seven churches] in His right hand, Who goes about among the seven golden lampstands [which are the seven churches]

WEJ-Paraphrase (Rev. 2:1)

> Though this is written to a specific church located in Ephesus near the first century, the truth contained here has relevance for every area of life for Christians, whether in marriage relationships or as a single set apart to God. This message is dear to God's heart. Please pay attention and let this truth change you spiritually.

AMP (Rev. 2:2)

> I know your industry and activities, laborious toil and trouble, and your patient endurance, and how you cannot tolerate wicked [men] and have tested and critically appraised those who call [themselves] apostles (special messengers of Christ) and yet are not, and have found them to be impostors and liars.

WEJ-Paraphrase (Rev. 2:2)

> You produce results; you apply yourself; you are never idle. You have at least enough love for God that you still hate evil.

AMP (Rev. 2:3)

I know you are enduring patiently and are bearing up for My name's sake, and you have not fainted or become exhausted or grown weary.

WEJ-Paraphrase (Rev. 2:3)

As you produced results for God, you also faced enemy attacks, and somehow you found a way to ride the wave of opposition directed at God's name and you did not give up.

AMP (Rev. 2:4)

But I have this [one charge to make] against you: that you have left (abandoned) the love that you had at first [you have deserted Me, your first love].

WEJ-Paraphrase (Rev. 2:4)

But you know there is one thing that really matters to me: your motivation in all you do must only and always be from the purest love for me, the kind of love you had for me when you first learned about my goodness. Back then, you easily received my agape love, and you loved me back with affection only my agape love can produce. Now, however, you produce results from some motivation other than your pure first love. I, the Lord, cannot compromise agape love for producing results (as mentioned in 1 Corinthians 13).

AMP (Rev. 2:5)

Remember then from what heights you have fallen. Repent (change the inner man to meet God's will) and do the works you did previously [when first you knew the Lord], or else I will visit you and remove your lampstand from its place, unless you change your mind and repent.

6 WHAT IS A HONEYMOON REALLY SUPPOSED TO BE?

WEJ-Paraphrase (Rev. 2:5)

Producing results by any means necessary does not meet my standard, says the Lord. You once cared about having a pure motivation of agape love. So stop what you are doing and change your ways. This is urgent. FIRST, remember the pure love you once had for me, the Lord. SECOND, repent by agreeing with me that you have lost your way, lost your first love for me. Nothing else matters to me. OR ELSE, if you don't act promptly, you will lose everything you think you have secured. There is danger right around the corner that you will not be able to withstand because you have lost my most powerful agent, my agape love. You will know you have truly repented when any further work you do for me is motivated and fueled by agape love (not this masquerade you have going on).

AMP (Rev. 2:6)

Yet you have this [in your favor and to your credit]: you hate the works of the Nicolaitans [what they are doing as corrupters of the people], which I Myself also detest.

WEJ-Paraphrase (Rev. 2:6)

You can repent and change; do not believe it is hopeless. You can return to your first love. That you have withstood the deceptive tools and techniques found in the heretical message of the Nicolaitans are a sign to me and should be encouragement to you that you can still repent, if you take my warning seriously.

AMP (Rev. 2:7)

He, who is able to hear, let him listen to and give heed to what the Spirit says to the assemblies (churches). To him who overcomes (is victorious), I will grant to eat [of the fruit] of the tree of life, which is in the paradise of God.

WEJ-Paraphrase (Rev. 2:7)

This is a spiritual warning; the alarm will not register to you on an emotional, financial, or social level. Allow your spirit to hear the deep, drumming alarm and run back to Me immediately. You can overcome this because I say so. If you believe Me, then you will come back to your first love for Me, and we will be together one day in my paradise.

To go deeper on section 6.3,
Visit www.ThePowerOfAHoneymoon.com/phmtools

Writing Activity 6.4

- 6.4.1. After reviewing God's perspective on having a first love for Him and allowing that to be the sole source of any good thing we produce, are there practical benefits this passage can offer for your marriage or your future marriage?

  _____
  _____

- 6.4.2. From your reading, why does the quality of motivation for doing things matter so much to God the Father?

  _____
  _____

- 6.4.3. Did Jesus pass the test of having a first love for God when He was on earth and living with His disciples?

Yes____ / No____, If no, why?_____

- 6.4.4. If yes, how did He succeed in it?

  _____
  _____

- 6.4.5. How is being wholehearted or prayerful beneficial in living out this first love?

_____

_____

To go deeper on section 6.4,
Visit www.ThePowerOfAHoneymoon.com/phmtools

❋ ❋ ❋

Blueprint Six Summary

A summary of Blueprint VI is found in Revelations 2:4, 2:1-7.

God gives us significant documentation on how to experience a life that enables us to give and receive love so that we can succeed in loving to His standards, and even on how to make necessary corrections along the way.

Part 1 of 3, Agape love is the highest quality of love that has always been in existence since the beginning, and it is the singular fuel that can make all relationships succeed, in particular, in making the relationship between husband and wife thrive without divorce. (1 Cor. 13)

Part 2 of 3, The accountability demonstrated in the Garden of Eden towards Adam and Eve will similarly reoccur after this life finishes. (Gen. 3:17; Rev. 2:4)

Part 3 of 3, God shows us His blueprint for our relationship with Him. When we marry, He shows us the way to a relationship with our spouse, specifically how He has designed us to experience the intangible oneness. Lastly, God gives us hands-on guidance on how to operate in our optimal design. God doesn't hold back on any significant details, even giving us an extended glimpse of the approach He will take during the review of our love and living while we were on earth. All of this is to encourage us to the pathway to thriving in the world that is still His! (Rev. 2:1–7)

Keeping the Pursuit of First Love for God in Marriage

What is The One Thing that Helped Elyssa Determine to Keep Pursuing First Love for God in Marriage?

"I had to go all in," she said. "I couldn't hold back some reserves for myself. Emotional vulnerability hasn't come easy to me in the past. But being fully emotionally transparent and invested, going all in, allowed me to fully experience this authentic marriage blueprint."

What is The One Thing That Helped Wladimir Determine to Keep Pursuing First Love for God in Marriage?

"The one most significant thing that changed my marriage life was to love my wife through practicing prayer like I had never known before. Without the daily discipline of prayer for my spouse spurned on by *The Power of a Praying® Husband* booklet by Stormie Omartian, I would not have known how to be the kind of husband to my bride Elyssa that Jesus is to the church! My prayers keep my heart tender toward my bride and sensitive toward the Holy Spirit's leading and direction. Prayer is what gives us a passionate unity of body, heart, mind, and soul. Lastly, prayer makes me a strong and vigilant protector of my marriage against outside, foreign attacks of the one enemy."

An Opportunity to Celebrate Is Awaiting

Revelation 2 is very applicable to marriages. Never believe that the googly-eyed love you once had for each other was an immature love you need to outgrow. When you lose your way and forget what it meant to love your spouse with that googly-eyed love, stop, double-and-triple-check your googly-eyed in love for God is operational. Then do acts to your spouse from your heart full of love—this takes you back to the way things were when you first loved in your relationship. These acts will help you find a way to fall crazy in love with each other again.

Chapters 3 through 6 covered the Scriptures we have used to propel us along our path of revolutionary dating and now marriage. We don't believe we have unique genes, luck, or ambitions that set us apart to be God honoring during our dating, entering into our marriage and now thriving as married. Rather, with deep humility, we sought out the truth of God's guidance on marriage, love, singlehood, and dating. God has revealed Himself to us in our seeking, and He has answered the door when we knocked. He has shared His truth with us about love and relationships, and now we have shared it with you. Enjoy the race marked out for your revolutionary love and marriage.

In the Chapters 7 through 11, we share our stories. On we go!

7 THE HONEYMOON-LIVING HUSBAND

In this book, we are documenting what can happen when two Christ followers (my beautiful bride and I) take to heart God's guidance through Scripture and His Holy Spirit for the chaotic world of dating, love, and authentic marriage. We hope our example stirs others to experience singlehood, dating, and love relationships in a radical and extravagant way. We document some of our key choices and the results we experienced that were meaningful in our journey of finding God-honoring love in dating and marriage. In this and the following two chapters (Chapter 8: The Honeymoon Wife and Chapter 9: Honeymoon Living) we uncover only the tip of the iceberg in how we (and others) are growing in our unshakable trust in God, in His authentic dating and marriage blueprint, in each other, and in the abundant fruit-filled life that our marriage (or others' marriages) will produce.

Throughout this chapter, I will share stories of several experiences that propelled me toward becoming a *honeymoon living single* man and then a honeymoon living husband. Similarly, in Chapter 8, my loving bride does the same, laying out her stories of becoming a *honeymoon living single* woman while we were dating and then becoming the honeymoon living wife she is now. Also, in this and the following chapters, we will discuss the key choices we made in the year-plus leading up to our wedding and the experiences we have had since our wedding in fulfilling our lofty vows. On our journey toward a honeymoon living life, my bride and I made seven leaps.

Honeymoon Living Singlehood and Marriage Leaps

1. **Cultivate a first love for God and watch it grow and empower you.** *(Covered here and in Chapter 8.)*

2. Eradicate all obstacles that prevent living a life of passion, purity and connectedness. *(Covered here and in Chapter 10.)*

3. Grow in your knowledge of the authentic dating and marriage blueprint from the Bible. *(Covered in Chapters Three through Six.)*

4. Husbands and wives be empowered by the fullness of your shared calling on your marriage, or when single be empowered by your full life calling. *(Covered in an upcoming book in this series.)*

5. Receive the freedom presented in your role in your marriage, or when single in your single life. *(Covered in an upcoming book in this series.)*

6. Receive from God daily the strategy to fully understand, love, and appreciate your spouse and fully be understood, loved and appreciated by your spouse. While single, thrive in God's unique work for you and be empowered by His unlimited strength daily. *(Covered in an upcoming book in this series.)*

7. Develop a single or married life that is appreciated and desired by others because of the appealing beauty that shines from it. *(Covered in Chapter 9.)*

✱ ✱ ✱

The year-plus leading up to marriage was built on intense learning about God from an average of forty-five minutes of daily prayer and Scripture reading. This in-depth, personal Scripture study was on top of three-plus years of annually reading the Bible from cover-to-cover. This is how I got started as a pre-honeymoon husband (*a honeymoon living single man*) and how I became primed for the honeymoon living journey.

To go deeper on the Honeymoon Living Leaps,
   Visit www.ThePowerOfAHoneymoon.com/phmtools

How Radical Is Growing in Scripture?

Without that in-depth, daily searching in Scripture, I would not have been tender to God's prompting to learn more about modeling with Actors, Models, and Talent for Christ (AMTC).

Studying Scripture will cause you to grow in your knowledge of God's nature and goodness.

On Sunday, July 29, 2013, God spoke to me: "Hey, remember that AMTC billboard that you first noticed a month ago and now see weekly during your commute to church? That billboard is for you. Now go join AMTC." The next day during my lunch break, I got on the AMTC website, and to my surprise, I discovered that they were holding auditions in Chicago (where I was living at the time) that weekend.

Was it the voice of vain pursuit that told me I should learn how to model at age thirty-seven? Or was it God leading me toward activities that would be a waste of my time and money? No. Instead, as I prayed and studied Scripture each day, I grew in my honeymoon love (or a first love) for God and learned more about the various gifts He placed in me. He wanted me to seek opportunities to use them for His glory.

I auditioned with AMTC the following Saturday, August 3, 2013, and was accepted into their modeling and acting training program. Fast-forward sixty-eight days: I was matched on eHarmony® with Elyssa on October 10, 2013. Later, my bride told me that seeing my professional (AMTC) modeling photos on eHarmony® helped me to stand out from the other eHarmony® matches.

I knew God wanted me to explore modeling as a vehicle to use my appearance for His good name, but what could give me the confidence I needed since I didn't have a creative circle of friends encouraging or affirming me? Leap one toward honeymoon living is to actually have a preeminent, "first before all" love for God. Then, skipping and jumping to leap three, we must cultivate our first love for God through quality, focused time dedicated to knowing Him, followed by obedience to the things we learn and the direction He leads. Through these two leaps, God helped me understand His good intentions for me and led me to choose His path into the unchartered territory of modeling at thirty-seven years old. When God said, "Hey, go learn to be a model, go learn acting," He was actually setting me up to be an outstanding match on eHarmony® to none other than the red-headed, modelesque, six-foot-one inch Elyssa, who lived 1,200 miles and a 24-hour car trip away.

Growing in Scripture Will Cause You to Obey or Surrender to God's Voice

I was excited about God and wanted to serve His kingdom. I became involved in with a large church community in June 2012. I made a commitment to God that I would plant every seed He gave me. So at church I began to participate in exciting work cultivating a "small church" community within a large church, just like our tagline said: "Making Big Church Small." It was a great idea, and I showed enthusiasm and interest in it. I had moved to Illinois ten years prior to train for the church pastorate. However, at that current time, my full-time occupation was building software applications and delivering technical solutions.

So began my silent standoff with God. I was over qualified to be a lay church leader, but I resisted God's prompting to become officially invested in that church by being a part-time pastor. I was already doing leadership work without even being asked because I am naturally gifted to shepherd and pastor. But I told God I would not take on professional pastoring and shepherding work without having a wife.

The years were ticking by, and I was still single. In two years, I would be facing forty. I knew giving God ultimatums is unnecessary, immature, and even dangerous. But was I really saying to God that I would resist serving Him at a pastoral level until He gave me a wife? In the spring of 2013, four months before being matched with Elyssa on eHarmony®, I gave God an option that I never remember giving Him previously. As I prepared to turn thirty-eight, I said, "Is it possible that You called me to be single forever?"

He said, "Yes, it is possible, would you still be willing to follow Me?"

"Yes, even in this I will follow Your plan," I told Him, going all in with God. I immediately withdrew my standoff ultimatum and went willingly to Him, even depending on Him to provide the strength I would need to live as a life-long single person; if that is what He wanted. From that moment, I made known my candidacy for the part-time pastor position. *(Leap Three: even if you aren't married, cultivate God's calling on your life by getting involved in a work or transforming your existing passion to be a vehicle for serving God.)* I am grateful God accepted my willingness to be single for the rest of my life and then promoted me with a call to marriage—that is what He intended for me all along.

Once again, His Scriptures struck! This act of surrender to His will is captured in my journal. From Friday, June 14, through Monday, June 17, I was studying Jesus' entry into ministry in Matthew 1:18-25, which follows after Jesus was baptized by John and led into the wilderness. Jesus begins His preaching ministry in Verse 17 and shortly afterwards selects His disciples. These events in the life of Jesus brought blinding clarity to me for honeymoon-living as a single or spouse: I had to be willing to forgo getting married (or any other desire I was holding onto) truly to serve God.

God used the depiction of Jesus choosing His disciples as a way to tell me that I had been "promoted." He assured me He had called me to be married, and it was particularly important that I ask of Him a wife in order to do more of God's work rather than just to assuage my loneliness. From that moment, I knew God gave me the green light to look for my wife. Nothing could hold me back.

Learning Dating per God's Blueprint for Dating, And More

Fast-forward almost a year; Elyssa accepted my proposal to begin officially courting on April 1, 2014. During that time, Scripture gave me one last nuclear strike for becoming a *honeymoon-living single male*. God was calling me to recommit to a life of purity and to becoming a rededicated spiritual virgin (that story is covered in Chapter 10: Honeymoon Revolution: Singles Roadmap).

My bride has been a staff member for many years at DaniJohnson.com. Dani of DaniJohson.com is a globally renowned business, finance, and relationship expert and coach. My bride coordinates logistics for events, negotiates contracts with hotels, and provides talent development at this company. She also travels multiple times a year with the company for these conferences. We first met during the DaniJohnson.com business-training event called "First Steps to Success" in Baltimore on May 3, just a few weeks after our official courtship began. Meeting her in person after months of Skype and Google Hangout was significant. However, because she was a busy professional who often traveled, meeting up while she was "on duty" was our best choice for our first and subsequent long-distance dates. In addition, Dani Johnson, Elyssa's mentor and friend of fifteen years, was going to be inspecting me indirectly, as well.

Prior to meeting Elyssa, I had a conviction against having pre-marital sex (which I mentioned on eHarmony®), but I had no conviction against pre-marital kissing. That was challenged at the DaniJohnson.com First Steps event. As part of the finale of the event, the staff recognition, Dani gave her customary praise of Elyssa as being a great staff member. Then she went further, "Elyssa is a virgin, and no one will touch her virgin lips until her wedding day." Elyssa and I had not yet had a conversation about kissing. Even though Dani and I hadn't met, she knew Elyssa's boyfriend was in the audience. Though said in front of more than a thousand conference attendees, I took this as said for my benefit and an indirect challenge. I was wowed; however, I was not scared of high standards and wasn't spooked by her rule for Elyssa. Although I later learned that Elyssa wasn't 100 percent sure she was committed to the no-kissing-till-wedding day conviction.

No rush. Kissing Elyssa didn't have to be sorted out on the first weekend we met in person. However, we did start talking about the pluses and minuses of our predicament. I wouldn't mind kissing or not kissing while we were dating. But either way we chose, it had to be mine and Elyssa's conviction and not just her mentor's. This was the only requirement I had.

Later that same month, we had a second date in Georgia, and we didn't kiss. A week later, we had another meetup on my home turf in Chicago.

My bride was becoming more open to the idea of kissing before marriage, and I invited her to keep an open mind. But I didn't want her feel forced by my preference that we just kiss when we feel the time is right. However, continuing my daily Scripture study, I began to sense God. He prompted me that my view was not part of His authentic blueprint for dating.

Between our visits in Georgia and Chicago, Elyssa had reversed course on the matter of kissing, but so had I. I was studying Matt 5:27–30, and Scripture told me clearly that kissing before marriage would lead to danger for our relationship. I accepted the terms given by the Spirit, and I decided I would no longer add fuel to the fire when the topic of kissing came up with Elyssa. However, I also hadn't made known to her my new conviction from Scripture that we should not kiss before we met at the altar.

Here are the Scripture passages and notes taken from my journal during that time.

God's Blueprint for Premarital Kissing and Sex: Matthew 5:27–30

Can God have an Opinion on Sex or Kissing during Singlehood and Dating?

Without asking this question, then I would have been miserable creating an arbitrary blueprint for sex or kissing during dating. Below is the passage that answered the question.

I invite you to peruse The Scriptures, using your Bible or one online. I will use The Amplified® Bible Translation, (AMP). Then I will make a summary observation of the scripture passage verse by verse, which will be labeled "WEJ-Paraphrase."

AMP (Matt. 5:27)

You have heard that it was said, You shall not commit adultery.

WEJ-Paraphrase (Matt. 5:27)

What did the seventh commandment say about adultery? The literal meaning is inadequate, and one needs the spiritual meaning. You shall not take possession of another person's belonging. Who owns everything but God? Then do not get comfortable trespassing on the domain of God because you are on shaky ground.

AMP (Matt. 5:28)

But I say to you that everyone who so much as looks at a woman with evil desire for her has already committed adultery with her in his heart.

WEJ-Paraphrase (Matt. 5:28)

Any person who looks at a member of the opposite sex who is not a spouse and arouses the desire to have a sexual encounter has committed adultery; whether or not physical contact occurred.

AMP (Matt. 5:29)

If your right eye serves as a trap to ensnare you or is an occasion for you to stumble and sin, pluck it out and throw it away. It is better that you lose one of your members than that your whole body be cast into hell (Gehenna).

WEJ-Paraphrase (Matt. 5:29)

When you look at something to appreciate, and you find you cannot appreciate it without it taking hold of you, than forgo attempting to appreciate it. Instead, value your calling and goals over the temporary things that bind you and distract you. Otherwise, your temporary gratification will lead you straight to hell!

AMP (Matt. 5:30)

And if your right hand serves as a trap to ensnare you or is an occasion for you to stumble and sin, cut it off and cast it from you. It is better that you lose one of your members than that your entire body should be cast into hell (Gehenna).

WEJ-Paraphrase (Matt. 5:30)

If the acts you do with your hands cause you to sin with a woman (i.e. if touching her creates arousal equal to that of a husband and wife though you are not married to her) than you will be granting a foothold to the enemy that can take you straight to hell. Stay sober and solemn about everything that naturally could lead to a stronghold of the enemy!

* * *

Prerequisites to True Honeymoon Living Singlehood

Elyssa had come to my Chicago turf, and I was poised to take a stand, because only a few days prior I had discovered God's blueprint for dating. Elyssa and I were at the Chicago Botanic Garden. It was a sunny day, and we were on a picnic blanket on a lush, green lawn. The conversation turned toward kissing, and this is when and where our first kiss could have happened. However, with total transparency and confidence in Scripture, I communicated my new conviction that we shouldn't kiss while we were still unmarried. I told her about my study in Matthew, how we belong to God, and would be trespassing on God's property if we were to kiss and arouse sexual passion in each other. When I finished talking, my bride welcomed the news and supported God's guidance in this completely. Our simple response to what God is teaching the passage:

- Elyssa was not yet my wife, and therefore, she wholly belongs to the Lord. She cannot give herself to me until God gives her the clearance. Then God will give me the clearance to receive her as His provision from Him to steward, love and be ultimately held accountable to Him for her.

- I was not yet her husband, and therefore, I belonged to the Lord, too.

- God had entrusted to me to guide spiritually our relationship towards honor at the standard set by God.

- God showed me the higher way in the choice of whether to kiss or not to kiss her.

- God would give us the strength to keep our resolve if we agreed with His viewpoints. But if we didn't wholeheartedly agree with Him, then we would not find His strength to overcome the temptation and choose His best for our relationship.

For multimedia companion on this section 7, #Purity-Victory
Visit www.ThePowerOfAHoneymoon.com/phmmedia

God provided the way of escape through Scripture for our good and for blessings in our relationship. Incidentally, during Elyssa's trip to Chicago, within 48-hours of the time on those green lawn and executing God's dating blueprint, God sealed the deal in her heart that I was called to be her husband.

We not only received guidance from the Lord for a higher way; we also had strength to walk away and never have that conversation or struggle about kissing again until our wedding. We had three more visits together while we were dating: (AMTC modeling debut in Orlando, Florida, where we were next door neighbors and had long schedules at the AMTC Summer Shine on July 4; my grandma's funeral on Long Island in early August; and Labor Day Weekend in Sonora, California, to visit Elyssa's family), and God allowed us to confidently enjoy each other and reap special favor for our long distance dating. During a fourth trip, (an October First Steps To Success conference in Cincinnati, Ohio), I proposed.

For multimedia companion on this section 7, #4thVisitAndTheProposal
Visit www.ThePowerOfAHoneymoon.com/phmmedia

7 THE HONEYMOON-LIVING HUSBAND

Growing According To Scripture Will Help You Know the Will of God and Preserve God's Intended Blessings in Dating and Love

The last two ways Scripture revolutionized our dating relationship and propelled us into marriage are evident in our custom wedding vows. The Genesis creation story (Gen 2 - 3:24) and Apostle Paul's teaching in Ephesians 5:21-32 became very important passages for us both in the months before our wedding. I would later write my wedding vows from the truth I wrestled out of these two Scripture passages (covered in more detail in Chapters 3 through 6). *This activity of building our custom wedding vows on God's authentic blueprint is an example of leap five to becoming a honeymoon living husband.*

Not surprising, both Elyssa's vows and mine were steeped in Scripture and filled with the truths that ignited our passion, commitment, and focus. Any Christian single or already married person can rediscover God's unique blueprint for marriage by reviewing the Scriptures we used in our vows. Particularly, they provide guidance on the specific roles of husband and wife. We know that it was this foundation of Scripture that tenderized our hearts to grow in wisdom, courage, and freedom in God; to develop our love to the purest, highest form; and to seek to nurture each other (such as not kissing before marriage but seeking to honor God in our relationship over our desires).

Confident Husbandhood: Ephesians 5:25–29

> "^{25} *Husbands, love your wives, as Christ loved the church and gave Himself up for her,* ^{26} *So that He might sanctify her, having cleansed her by the washing of water with the Word,* ^{27} *That He might present the church to Himself in glorious splendor, without spot or wrinkle or any such things [that she might be holy and faultless].* ^{28} *Even so husbands should love their wives as [being in a sense] their own bodies. He who loves his own wife loves himself.* ^{29} *For no man ever hated his own flesh, but nourishes and carefully protects and cherishes it, as Christ does the church*" (Eph. 5:25-29).

Wladimir's Custom Wedding Vows

Elyssa, my vows come from my learning of what is and how to be a husband based on the picture portrayed in the Book of Ephesians, Chapter 5, verses 25-29.

Verse 25 reads, "Husbands, love your wives, as Christ loved the church and gave Himself up for her."

{v25} Elyssa, I noticed this as the clearest example of a husband's love for his bride—Christ's example propels me to demonstrate a total and selfless care and love for you.

{v26} This love I pray will be expressed through my life-giving actions and words. Just as Christ's actions and words brought new life to His bride, I aspire, with God's help, to do nothing to diminish you from who Christ has made you and is in the process of perfecting you to be.

Verse 27 reads, "That He might present the church to Himself in glorious splendor, without spot or wrinkle or any such things [that she might be holy and faultless]."

{v27} Yes, my duty to you is lofty, and it will never be completed on earth. Nevertheless, Elyssa, I will perpetually look to our heavenly Father to be Christ-like in my love for you and to present you to God in the fashion as He intended.

{v28} Elyssa, the way God is joining us today is as us being one body. Hallelujah!!! Therefore, I vow to always consider you in every way as I consider myself.

As verse 29 noted, "For no man ever hated his own flesh, but nourishes and carefully protects and cherishes it, as Christ does the church,"

I deeply love you today, and I vow to love you more daily (especially since you are my own body now).

I vow to nourish you daily by supporting your needs and God's vision for you.

I vow to protect you daily by shielding you from physical and spiritual harm.

I vow to cherish you daily as my love, sweetness heart pie, and best friend and always shower you with words of affirmation, passion, and deeds of love.

In front of these witnesses, and with no exceptions, I vow to submit my will to Christ, to grow in all of God's Scriptures, and to grow my love for you, and I promise before God and you to put no other thing or person before you except our Lord and Savior.

All I vow today I will accomplish through the nourishing the Bible and the grace and power of God our Father, Jesus our Savior, and His Holy Spirit. I love you. And thank you for loving me!

For multimedia companion on this section 7, #HusbandsWeddingVows Visit www.ThePowerOfAHoneymoon.com/phmmedia

* * *

Confidence for a Husband to Fulfill Vows for a Lifetime

After I read my vows at the wedding, Elyssa's 85-year-old Grandpa Williams came up to me and said, *"You promised a lot in those vows."*

I responded back, *"Yeah, I did, but I love her."*

My response to him was beyond emotionalism, heroics, or theatrics. I was not taken back by my 85-year-old beloved new grandpa in-law about the depth and sincerity of my vows. Since, I had learned about 1 Corinthians 13 unfathomable love fuel. God provides this agape fuel for the husband, and it showed its effectiveness in Jesus's life. Jesus thoroughly loved with agape in the close quarters of Him and the disciples. He nurtured them while He maintained the focus on doing God's calling to completion. Jesus lived a life of prayer dependence where God empowered Jesus to fulfill His call and nurture His bride (the church), which started with successfully nurturing His disciples. Jesus modeled living in agape love, and we can imitate this love as husband and wife. My confidence to fulfill my vows was not in my strength, but I had a deep sense God didn't make marriage to be a losing proposition but rather a stance to win at life. I had confidence in God's design of marriage and His agape-love resource to succeed, along with Jesus' giving us marriage-like demonstration to follow-through to our own marriage success. Yay God!

I have dedicated significant space in this book to spell out the important principles in my journey leading up to marriage, and those exact same principles have continued to play out in our marriage. A honeymoon dating relationship and a honeymoon marriage share these same seven leaps.

Recap of The Honeymoon Living Singlehood and Marriage Leaps

1. Cultivate a first love for God and watch it grow and empower you. *(Covered here and in Chapter 8.)*

2. Eradicate all obstacles that prevent living a life of passion, purity and connectedness. *(Covered here and in Chapter 10.)*

3. Grow in your knowledge of the authentic dating and marriage blueprint from the Bible. *(Covered in Chapters Three through Six.)*

4. Husbands and wives be empowered by the fullness of your shared calling on your marriage, or when single be empowered by your full life calling. *(Covered in an upcoming book in this series.)*

5. Receive the freedom presented in your role in your marriage, or when single in your single life. *(Covered in an upcoming book in this series.)*

6. Receive from God daily the strategy to fully understand, love, and appreciate your spouse and fully be understood, loved and appreciated by your spouse. While single, thrive in God's unique work for you and be empowered by His unlimited strength daily. *(Covered in an upcoming book in this series.)*

7. Develop a singles or married life that is appreciated and desired by others because of the appealing beauty that shines from it. *(Covered in Chapter 9).*

※ ※ ※

In the end, God's blueprint will be the only requirement any Christ follower (husband, wife, or single) will be held accountable to live out in marriage or singlehood. Fortunately, God's ingenious blueprint is discernible to whosoever would give Him the space to speak to them on this subject. His plans can be discerned and followed through the Holy Spirit's help. Then dating and marriage will be as awesome as He meant it to be. The truths my bride and I received and wrote into our vows are the essence of God's terms for how to succeed in marriage. We can give credit only to God and continue to learn from His manifesto on love leaked out to us through the pages of Scripture.

We believe the good things that are growing out of our love for God and went into our singlehood, our dating, and now our married life can start a revolution in someone else's life. We will share our story hoping others will share the good things growing out of their love for God and contribute to the start of a dating and marriage revolution.

8 THE HONEYMOON-LIVING WIFE

I always wanted to get married, or at least assumed I would get married. I think I just figured I would just stumble onto the right guy one day. After all, I was active in my local community, I had a great career, I had done global ministry, I had met thousands of people from all over the world. But somehow my entire twenties had passed me by, and not one dragon-slaying, handsome prince charming had showed up on a white horse.

Facing Reality: 30 and Still Single

On my thirtieth birthday, I decided to take the entire day off work so I could spend substantial time with the Lord and enjoy a day of some of my favorite things. It was on my thirtieth birthday that I got smacked with a 2x4 of reality.

A mentor and friend of mine, Dani Johnson invited me out to lunch for my birthday. (This is the same Dani from Chapter 7, the globally renowned business, finance, and relationship expert and coach). Over our lunch conversation, she challenged me about my life, specifically about whether I wanted to get married or dedicate my life to being single.

For multimedia companion on this section 8, #FacingThirty
Visit www.ThePowerOfAHoneymoon.com/phmmedia

The conversation went something like this:

"Elyssa, you have walked in purity your entire life; you have never been sexually intimate with a man. You have a rare gift. It's beautiful. Since you aren't married, you don't have the pulls and distractions on your life that come from being married. Being married and having children is a wonderful thing, but do you actually want to be married?"

"Did I actually want to get married?" I was surprised at her question. Wasn't the answer obvious?

She continued, *"My husband and kids are my greatest gifts in the world. I love them completely. I am not trying to talk you out of marriage if that is what you are really called to and desire. But are you sure that you are called to be a wife? Or do you actually want to dedicate your whole life solely to God and remain single?"*

Her words challenged my mindset.

"Figure out if you actually want to be married. Search it out, and figure out if you are actually called to be single. Do you want to be married because you think it's something that you should do, that's been programmed into since you were young?"

Then it hit me. My culture had taught me that I was *supposed* to get married. We all live with certain expectations placed on us. Not all of us are raised in environments where marriage is expected. Some of us are raised to believe that advanced education or career or family legacy are of utmost importance. But where I was raised—in a small-town, tight-knit community—marriage was expected. I was just sixteen years old when my friends started getting married, and they just kept on getting married after I was out of my teens and all through my twenties. I would get invitation after invitation to weddings. I was always a bridesmaid, never the bride (or I was the maid of honor, the guestbook hostess, the wedding planner, the emcee, the cake server, the punch re-filler, the "stay and clean up the reception hall when it's all over and drive home alone" girl).

Since I was a young child, I had seen movies where prince charming and the princess meet, get married, and live happily ever after. Since I was a young child, people had talked about my husband as if we were already married. The older I got, the more people asked about him, "*So are you seeing anybody special?"* *"When are you going to tie the knot?"* Then I got a little older, and the comments were more spiteful, *"You're not getting any younger you know."* *"You wouldn't understand dearie; you aren't married."* *"You're still single!"* *"Don't worry dear, your turn will come"*

I graciously listened to their comments for years, always with a smile, but inwardly I was saying, *"Stop it! Stop belittling me because my life doesn't look the way you think it should. Please stop telling me that I have to have a man to complete me. Stop telling me that I am broken. Just stop it. Stop judging me, stop putting pressure on me."*

All of it flashed through my head as Dani posed her questions: prince charming programming, the expectations, the pressure to do life the way "they" thought I should.

Then Dani said, *"You know, you aren't less of a woman if you don't get married."*

I lost it and broke down crying right there in the nicest restaurant in town. Tears were streaming down my face.

"Why are you crying?" Dani asked.

"Because nobody has ever said that," I told her. *"Nobody has ever given me permission to be just me and for it to be enough."*

"You aren't less if you decide to dedicate your entire life to a different pursuit. It's just a different call."

Smack! That was the 2x4. I had grown up and assumed by default I was going to get married. Dani offered me permission to *not* do the thing that culture and myself were demanding of me.

Before we went our separate ways, Dani and I prayed together that God would reveal to me what His will was for my life and if I was in fact called to be single or to get married. And if God was asking me to be single, we prayed that I would be willing to walk that path with diligence, contentment, obedience, and joy for a lifetime.

I left lunch that day and handed my life over to the Lord in a new way. I fully gave him my dream of being married and everything that that meant: a life together with another, somebody to have kids with, and someone to change the world with, a man to go to bed with at night and wake up to in the morning, that special person I could build my dreams with and help him build his. In a world where everybody around me kept getting married, could I live alone with contentment? Could I really trust God to that level? I surrendered it all. That dedication meant I had to be willing even to live without marital intimacy for my entire life.

I cried out to God, *"Wait, no sex ever? Nobody to sit on a porch swing with when I get old? Nobody? I have honored you my entire life; I haven't even kissed anybody, and I am thirty years old! I mean, come on God, really? Are you going to require of me to live such an extreme life that I don't ever get to be kissed, that I never get to have sex, and that I live life single forever?"*

So I died to the dream. I gave it to God. I had always had a secret plan of what my ideal timing for marriage should look like. I wanted a wedding by age twenty-one. When that didn't happen, I kept moving the timeline to twenty-three, twenty-five, twenty-seven, twenty-nine. I wanted to get married on my timeline, in my way. Sure, I was radical by culture's standards in the way I held myself to high standards in regards to sex, not dating around because I believed that God would bring the right man in His timing. I was genuine in my resolve to trust God, and I was determined not to settle for anything less than the best God had for me. But, I had a secret place in my heart that I still held onto, it was my timing. *I wanted God's timing to match mine.*

Let me say that again. Don't miss this. This is a major leap in living a honeymoon life and marriage: *I had a secret place in my heart that I still held control of.* I wanted to control God's timing. And it was easy to justify. I mean it wasn't a *bad* thing to want to get married in my twenties to an amazing man of God. But in my heart, I held my will higher than His. I wanted to control His timing. That is called an idol. And God hates idols. He wants all of us. He wants our whole heart. He wants us fully abandoned to him without secret places in our hearts held back for ourselves. What do you think of when you think of an idol? A big statue that people worship? A golden calf? An image of Buddha? A fancy car? A TV show?

I would suggest to you that idolatry is often sneakier and more "justifiable" than we give it credit for. If you have places in your heart where you are retaining control, you are going to have a hard time finding success in those areas. For me, one of those areas was my secret desire to control the timing of God for when I would get married. That was the root of a dangerous tree. I killed the root of control that day.

I chose on my thirtieth birthday to walk down the path of surrender. When that nasty idol of control was revealed to me, I surrendered it. I died to it. I died to the dream of getting married. I died to having the "right" to get married. I died to my "right" to control the timing. I died to the "right" to control how I would meet my husband. I had many genuinely good ideas of what that was supposed to look like, too. What I had to let go of, though, was *my plan*. My plan got me to thirty and single. The thing is, our plans will get us only so far. They might even get us to good places, but are our plans God's plans? His plans are beautiful. His plans will perfect us to His glory. His plans may seem like they take too long, but I would bet most of the times when we feel like His plans are taking too long, it's because we are fighting with Him over the steering wheel of our lives. Our plans are going to leave us in the desert much longer than we need to be.

The Path Called Surrender

Surrender isn't a one-time event. It's a daily, often moment-by-moment choice. We have to surrender to God and our spouses every day. When we fight that surrender, we put ourselves back into the driver's seat and grab the idol called control again. But the path of control is so painful. It happens so often around us and is so commonly justified that it seems normal. Being in control even seems right at times. It is all around us in our culture. The path that Wladimir and I have walked in our relationship and marriage is very different from what society is telling us. But society's track record speaks for itself, and we want no part of it. We want no part of the pain and mediocrity. We choose instead another path, a path with a successful track record.

Here is Jesus' Teaching on Marriage:

"And He answered and said, 'Have you not read that He who created them from the beginning made them male and female, and said, "For this reason a man shall leave his father and mother and be joined to his wife, and the two shall become one flesh"? So they are no longer two, but one flesh. What therefore God has joined together, let no man separate.' " (Matthew. 19:4-6, NASB)

That is a pretty strong statement. That is a high standard. It's God's standard.

I want to pause here before continuing that thought. I understand that many marriages are horrible, abusive, or even downright dangerous. I am not criticizing anyone in those situations. The last thing anybody dealing with a situation like that needs is judgment. I also realize that divorce is a common reality of many marriages. I am simply pointing out the vast differences between God's blueprint or design for marriage and culture's blueprint or design for marriage.

The Difference Between Heaven's Definition of Marriage and Culture's Definition

Do you know the difference between heaven's definition of marriage and culture's definition?

Heaven says, "You are one." ("...The two shall become one flesh.") (Matt. 19:5, NASB)
Culture says, "We are together when it's convenient."

Heaven says, "As long as you both shall live."
Culture says, "Until we divorce."

Heaven says, "What God has joined together, let no man separate."

Culture says, "Sign this prenuptial agreement."

Heaven says, "My love and commitment is unconditional."
Culture says, "My love and commitment is contingent on these items…"

Heaven says, "This union is a divine covenant, unbreakable and lasting."
Culture says, "This is a contract. If you do this and this and this, then I agree to do this and this, but not this or this."

Heaven says, "I lay down my life for you. I die for you. Daily."
Culture says, "You inconvenience me."

Heaven says, "I choose you forever. You're my one and only."
Culture says, "It's okay to window shop."

Heaven says, "I give myself fully to you."
Culture says, "I have the right to withhold myself from you."

Activity 8.1

What are additional truths that heaven declares over your current marriage now, or if single, your future marriage?

_____
_____
_____
_____

To go deeper on section 8.1,
  Visit www.ThePowerOfAHoneymoon.com/phmtools

Heaven Matches Wladimir and Elyssa

One year after my lunch with Dani, on June 14, my thirty-first birthday, there was a man after God's heart living in Chicago, seeking God's face whether God was going to call him to be a husband or to be single. Just like I had, exactly one year earlier (to the day), though we hadn't yet met one another.

A few months later on October 10, 2013, we were "matched" on eHarmony®. We started communicating by late November and got to know each other through eHarmony® for the next couple of months. By late January we had our first FaceTime phone call, and by March 31, Wladimir asked if we could see each other exclusively, even though we hadn't yet met face-to-face! We had both been seeking God's will, but I still thought it was a little weird to say yes to having a boyfriend I had never actually seen in real life. I told him I would think about it.

April 1st and All Green Lights

The next day was April 1, and I called my parents. *"I have something to tell you, and it's not an April Fools' joke."*

As soon as I began to fill them in, my mom blurted out, *"I knew it! God told me a couple of months ago that you were talking to someone!"*

My dad proceeded to grill me for a while and then said, *"It's all green lights."*

I was a little stunned. *"What?"*

"Do you know what you do when you see a green light?" my dad asked.

"Drive?" I answered.

"Yes, drive. And if a light turns yellow or red, you wait and see if it turns green again. It's all green lights as of now. Call the man back and tell him yes."

I called Wladimir and said to yes being his girlfriend. A month later, we met for the first time face-to-face; five and half months later we were engaged; and eight weeks after that we were married!

8 THE HONEYMOON-LIVING WIFE

Love Can Be Scary, But It's an Exhilarating Ride

I think my biggest challenge in the year leading up to marriage was growing in vulnerability and trusting. Becoming fully vulnerable and trusting of my eventual husband Wladimir required me letting go of common fears surrounding trusting and being vulnerable. Planet earth is a scary place at times. We all hurt. We love and loose. Our hearts can get crushed. But we dust off the pieces of our broken hearts and tape them back together. We wipe away our tears, get busy, and move on. We all have a broken heart story—or ten. Maybe it was a love story gone wrong. Maybe it was the loss of someone we cared for. Maybe it was a betrayal. It's not *if* we encounter loss, but it's *what* we do with it. Will we allow it to hold us back and cripple us, or will we emerge as conquerors?

You have to let your spouse in even though it's frightening. They need all of you. Don't hold back fully giving yourself to your spouse. You are God's gift to them, and they are God's gift to you.

Opening up my heart enough to allow myself to really need Wladimir was a challenge. I was independent and successful, and while I wanted to fall in love and get married, I also was afraid I was going to mess up and get hurt. For the past several years I had lived a fairly public life, and I was frightened of the idea that it might all go bad and I'd get my heart crushed in front of everybody. What if I messed up? What if Wladimir wasn't whom I thought he was? My story of living radically dedicated to God, standing for purity, and being a virgin had been heard all over the United States and around the globe by hundreds of thousands of people. I was looked up to as a role model and an inspiration. I had mentored and counseled others for years. As soon as I said yes to dating Wladimir, I knew that the days of being able to date in anonymity were over. I arrived at crossroads after crossroads and chose vulnerability over self-guarded protection each time.

Embracing the Covering

Wladimir moved from Illinois to Texas six weeks after we were engaged and two weeks before we got married. We had arranged for him to stay at a friend's house until the wedding day, and we unpacked his belongings into my garage. That first night when he drove off to where he was staying, I felt a massive shift take place. I owned my own home and had always felt strong and safe as the owner and protector of it. But after he left that night, there was this unmistakable gap. I don't really know how to describe it, but there was this sense in the house that the protector and man of the house was gone. It was an undeniable shift; I was no longer okay on my own. I suddenly felt the need for something I had never needed to that extent before: the need for covering. Specifically, I felt the irrefutable need for Wladimir's spiritual covering. It had happened. It was time for me to step into place beside him and allow him to become my covering and head our home.

The Big Day: The Start of Forever

The wedding day arrived, the music played, the bride walked down the aisle and met the groom at the altar. They smiled with joy at each other. They exchanged rings and said their vows. They kissed, and life as a married couple began. All the planning was over, the flowers began to fade and the reception was but a blur.

The wedding takes place on a day; the marriage is every day. It takes place in the ins and outs of "for better, for worse, for richer, for poorer, in sickness, in health…" The reality of "What 'da heck did we just do? We signed up for forever with each other? Um… Wow. Okay, then, breathe, just breathe" sets in.

In the hustle and bustle of the daily chaos of life, jobs, and whatever else is going on in the midst of planning a wedding—all the countless details, the family members causing drama, having too much to do and never enough time—it is so easy to lose focus on the magnitude of what is taking place, the magnitude that two people are promising forever to each other. It can be a little daunting.

Know What You Are Promising

What are you vowing there at the altar? It is more than "till death do we part." (That is somewhat depressing if that's all it is.) Yes, you are promising forever, but it's more a question of what are you going to *do* between now and forever. Whether you are already married or are going to get married, it is vitally important to understand what you are promising. Otherwise, it is going to be really hard to fulfill your vows. News flash! If you don't know what you are promising, it's hard to live it out, and your marriage will become a head spin of disillusionment.

Wladimir and I decided to write our own custom vows (and not because we are super accomplished writers who have oodles of creativity dripping off our fingertips … or lots of extra time). We started talking about the importance of marriage early in our friendship and dating relationship and about how we both wanted a marriage that was revolutionary in thought and action. We wanted a marriage that wasn't limited to the reality of those around us; we wanted something record breaking. When I was writing my vows, I really pressed into the Lord to hear what He was saying about our marriage. I also had a sense that these vows, while they were mine to give my husband and live out for him, were not just for me. They were for other wives and future wives to give their husbands. These vows have changed the course of marriages. I have heard the most amazing stories from other women about how these vows changed them, redirected their marriages, and inspired them.

Elyssa's Custom Wedding Vows

> **Wladimir Jesus-Redeemed Joseph,** how the Lord has led our journeys and brought us together.
>
> I have been fashioned and created for you. To be the rib from your side. Called to be your helpmate. A reflection of the beauty and the grace of God to you. Crafted by God to be the one to stand with

you in life, in love, and in ministry. Today God joins us together in marriage to forge His plans for us.

From this day forth, I promise, with God's help to set you above all earthly others. I promise to treasure you as the priceless treasure that He has created you to be. I will receive you as heaven's gift to me and embrace you as my own. I will stand beside you and with you and will cheer for you. I will pray to be a reflection of His light to you. I shall receive you. Give myself to you. Seek after God and work to represent Him to you, our family, and the world around us.

Ephesians 5:1-2 says, "Therefore be imitators of God, as beloved children; and walk in love, just as Christ also loved you and gave Himself up for us, an offering and a sacrifice to God as a fragrant aroma."

We are called to be like Him, to walk with resolve in childlike faith, shrouded in love. With that command in mind, I recommit to pursue God radically for the rest of my life, to resolve in my heart to be a living, breathing representation of His love, grace, and mercy to the world. By His guidance, I will love extravagantly, live sacrificially, and pour out my life as a living sacrifice to point others to Him.

Ephesians 5:22-24 says, "Wives, be subject to your own husbands, as to the Lord. For the husband is the head of the wife, as Christ also is the head of the church, He Himself being the Savior of the body. But as the church is subject to Christ, so also the wives ought to be to their husbands in everything."

What an extravagant representation! How the King of the universe and the Savior of the world models right relationship! It is from that picture of His kingdom relationship that I commit myself to you.

Today I choose you. I choose you to be my head. I choose to step into your covering and to respect your leadership. With God's help, I will honor and submit to you. It is with joy that I step into place beside you. I promise to stand by and with you as long as God gives us breath. I promise to be yours and yours alone. I promise to be

> *your greatest cheerleader, your safe place, and your friend. I promise to love you with passion. I vow to pursue living a life modeling His kingdom relationship.*
>
> *Thank you for your love. Thank you for your protection and covering. You are a warrior worth following. You are my Braveheart.*
>
> *God's Plan A, Baby. Plan A.*

For multimedia companion on this section 8, #WifesWeddingVows Visit www.ThePowerOfAHoneymoon.com/phmmedia

* * *

Confidence for a Wife to Fulfill Vows for a Lifetime

These vows are based on Scripture from the story of Adam and Eve in Genesis 2:18-25 and from Ephesians 5, which speaks of the relationships between Christ and the heavenly Father and between Christ and the church and the correlation to marriage relationships. (If you need a little refresher on it, we covered it in Chapters 3 and 5).

Fully Embrace the Call

Ladies, embrace who you are. You are a feminine delight to your man. You are made in the image of God. You are called to reflect the beauty, grace, and splendor of God to your spouse, and you were designed to be *one* with your beloved spouse. Cheer him on and give yourself to him—fully. Fellas, receive that gift. Marvel in the creation that has been crafted for you. God has given her to you to help you so that together you can conquer the calling God has on your lives.

Christ Is Your Standard

Love and live sacrificially. There is no greater representation of love than the love of our heavenly Father and Jesus Christ. Let Him be your standard.

Ephesians 5:1-2 says, "Therefore be imitators of God, as beloved children; and walk in love, just as Christ also loved you and gave Himself up for us, an offering, and a sacrifice to God as a fragrant aroma." (Eph. 5:1-2, NASB)

The "S" Word - Submit

What does it really mean to submit? Depending on the culture you have been surrounded by and your personal life experience, submitting can be a daunting obstacle in marriage. There are many pastors, leaders, men, and women that practically shout out, "Submit women," in cavemen-like fashion. While these people may mean well and while there is truth to what they are saying, shouting, "Submit" sometimes isn't a very helpful word to the women caught in their wake. It often leaves women feeling unimportant, diminished, voiceless, and powerless—not the best combination for a loving, embracing honeymoon marriage.

What is God's Way?

What is the truth about submitting? When I was approaching marriage, I really sought the Lord's heart about submitting to my husband. **Here is a Honeymoon Living Key:** When you are looking for the truth, the best place to get answers is from God (so simple, but true). His Word and the guidance of the Holy Spirit are unequaled truth tellers. What does His Word say? "Wives, be subject to your own husbands, as to the Lord. For the husband is the head of the wife, as Christ also is the head of the church, He Himself being the Savior of the body. But as the church is subject to Christ, so also the wives ought to be to their husbands in everything." (Eph. 5:22-24, NASB)

Think about how Jesus Christ and the Heavenly father display right relationship. What an extravagant representation! How the King of the Universe and the Savior of the World model right relationship! It is on that truth that we must base our unity as married couples. To put it simply, Jesus is the representation of perfect love. A love that heals every wound. A love so immense that He bore the weight of the sins of the whole world on the cross to free us from sin and darkness and to empower us as joint heirs. With humility, He serves His bride. With love He waits for her and picks her up and positions her to walk alongside of Him. Jesus was obedient to His Father's will to free the world from the grip of the enemy through His death and resurrection. That is love. That is surrender. That is leadership. That is our example. It is *that love* that is "head of the church." It is that love that is our model for marriage. We as couples are to emulate that love—a full and utter surrender to the Lord, working in harmony and understanding with one another. And we are to live out that union in our marriages —in our surrender and submission as wives and in our loving and dying as husbands. The result is unity that brings freedom.

What Really Happened after the Wedding Ceremony?

I Had to Make Choices and Still Have to Make Choices Each Day

- *Will I be vulnerable? Will I hold back letting my husband know me fully in this moment?*

- *Will I share my weaknesses? What if I share my weaknesses and he tries to fix them or sees me as broken now?*

- *Will I give my absolute all and be fully abandoned?*

- *Will I surrender to fear today?*

- *Will I choose to walk with my husband as one under his covering, or will I rebel against what I promised?*

- *Will I live out a honeymoon marriage? Will I be full of love and connected in heart and radically abandoned?*

- *Will I deny myself?*

- *Will I honor my spouse and submit to him even if I think he is wrong?*

- *Will I look for ways to recognize and receive the love of my spouse? Will I look to give love to my spouse in the way he needs it?*

- *Will I be attentive to the Holy Spirit and do as He directs?*

- *Will I choose today to live life more radically surrendered than yesterday?*

※ ※ ※

Being the bride of my husband is amazing. It is a daily privilege and delight. It is the fulfillment of my longest dream. I found my warrior worth fighting with. At times, the battle has been fierce, but it is so worth pressing through to the other side. Wherever you are in your journey of love, remember that Wladimir and I cheer you on. But even more importantly, remember that you have a Father in heaven who cheers you on. He will never leave you or forsake you, and He will be faithful to accomplish the work that He has started in you

9 HONEYMOON LIVING

This chapter is a partial action plan for the authentic marriage blueprint based on Genesis 1–3, Ephesians 5, 1 Corinthians 13, Revelations 2:1-7, and the life of Jesus in the Gospels (though not covered in this book). Understanding the life of Jesus is critical to Honeymoon Living and we will cover this in future books and media in this series.

In this chapter, we will work through the above passages and watch a coherent and concise travel plan emerge with twelve guideposts marking the way along the honeymoon living path. The authentic blueprint journey began in Genesis with Adam and Eve, and using the twelve guideposts below, we will forge a straight path equally traversable for single and married people.

All Scriptures that are underlined or bolded are the foundations of the twelve guideposts. The underlined Scriptures represent parts of a guidepost while **the bolded Scriptures are complete guideposts.** *We also will introduce two additional passages: Hebrews 12:6 and Romans 8:14-15.*

The Honeymoon Living Blueprint

> "*15 And the Lord God took the man and put him in the Garden of Eden to tend and guard and keep it. And the Lord God commanded the man, saying, You may freely eat of every tree of the garden; But of the tree of the knowledge of good and evil and blessing and calamity you shall not eat, for in the day that you eat of it you shall surely die …*" *(Gen. 2:15-16).*

"*¹⁸Now the Lord God said, it is not good (sufficient, satisfactory) that the man should be alone; I will make him a helper (suitable, adapted, complementary) for him ... ²¹ And the Lord God caused a deep sleep to fall upon Adam; and while he slept, He took one of his ribs or a part of his side and closed up the [place with] flesh. ²²And the rib or part of his side which the Lord God had taken from the man He built up and made into a woman, and He brought her to the man. ²³ Then Adam said, This [creature] is now bone of my bones and flesh of my flesh; she shall be called Woman, because she was taken out of a man ... ²⁴ Therefore a man shall leave his father and his mother and shall become united and cleave to his wife, and they shall become one flesh ... ²⁵And the man and his wife were both naked and were not embarrassed or ashamed in each other's presence*" (Gen. 2:18, 21-23, 24-25).

"*¹ Now the serpent was more subtle and crafty than any living creature of the field which the Lord God had made. And he [Satan] said to the woman, Can it really be that God has said,*" (Gen. 3:1).

✳ ✳ ✳

"*²¹ Be subject to one another out of reverence for Christ (the Messiah, the Anointed One). ²² **Wives, be subject** (be submissive and adapt yourselves) to your own husbands as [a service] to the Lord ... "²⁵ **Husbands, love your wives**, as Christ loved the church and gave Himself up for her ...*" (Eph. 21-12, 25).

✳ ✳ ✳

"*⁷ Love bears up under anything and everything that comes, is ever ready to believe the best of every person, its hopes are fadeless under all circumstances, and **it endures everything [without weakening]**.
⁸ **Love never fails** [never fades out or becomes obsolete or comes to an end]*" (1 Cor. 13:7-8).

9 HONEYMOON LIVING

* * *

"*⁶ But without faith it is impossible to please and be satisfactory to Him. For whoever would come near to God must [necessarily] believe that God exists and that He is the rewarder of those who earnestly and diligently seek Him [out]*" (Heb. 12:6).

"*¹⁴ For all who are led by the Spirit of God are sons of God. ¹⁵ For [the Spirit which] you have now received [is] not a spirit of slavery to put you once more in bondage to fear, but you have received the Spirit of adoption [the Spirit producing sonship] in [the bliss of] which we cry, Abba (Father)! Father!*" (Rom. 8:14-15).

* * *

"*⁴ But I [The Lord] have this [one charge to make] against you: that you have left (abandoned) the love that you had at first [you have deserted Me, your first love]. ⁵ Remember then from what heights you have fallen. Repent (change the inner man to meet God's will) and do the works you did previously [when first you knew the Lord], or else I will visit you and remove your lampstand from its place, unless you change your mind and repent. ⁷* **To him who overcomes (is victorious), I will grant to eat [of the fruit] of the tree of life, which is in the paradise of God**" (Rev. 2:4-5, 7).

From the above verses emerge twelve guideposts. This summary of the authentic blueprint can help single or married people navigate the journey of Honeymoon Living. Genesis talks about building the **vehicle** of service to God via a life of marriage or a life of singlehood (i.e. while Adam was first alone and given the stewarding task to tend the garden). Ephesians speaks of the expert **driver**, using the perfect **fuel** of agape love found in 1 Corinthians 13. And in the end, we find the **destination** in Revelation.

Twelve Guideposts to Honeymoon Living

Genesis 1–3, [**Vehicle**]
1. Completed as Stewards (Gen. 2:7, 15, 18, 22; 1:28)
2. Leave (Gen. 2:24)
3. Cleave (Gen. 2:24)
4. Naked (Gen. 2:25)
5. Not Ashamed (Gen. 2:25)
6. On Guard (Gen. 3:1)

* * *

Ephesians 5 [**Driver**] (Assumes the life of Jesus in the Gospels)
7. Marriage Guidance from the Life of Jesus (Eph. 5:25)

* * *

1 Corinthians 13, [**Fuel**]
8. The Only One Standard of Love for Marriage Demystified (1 Cor. 13:7-8)

* * *

Hebrews 11; Romans 8 [**Travel Identification**]
9. Faith in God (Heb. 11:6)
10. Sonship and Discipleship (Rom. 8:14-17)

* * *

Revelation 2 [**Destination**]
11. Reward. The Final Goal and Cheat-Sheet (Rev. 2:4)
12. Celebration (Rev. 2:1-7)

9 HONEYMOON LIVING

This chapter focuses on honeymoon living which is based on having a preeminent, first-before-all love for God, therefore the single person or the married person who lives this way is honeymoon living.

We abbreviate the discussion of some of the guideposts in this chapter because they are covered in other books and media resources. The most critical ones are addressed, and lively examples from our lives are provided to help make these principles relatable, accessible, and non-theoretical. In the following section we broach some of the honeymoon living guideposts.

Guideposts Part I: The Battle Plan Against Disinformation

In the beginning, God made Adam and Eve from His image to share in His relational attributes and to be spiritual beings dependent on Him.

Adam was created first and then later completed with Eve. While Adam was alone, prior to Eve, God gave him the responsibility to steward or tend God's garden. Even now, God creates each of us, whether single or married, with His unique agenda for us while on earth.

God had a secondary agenda and so completed Adam with Eve to fulfill that unique secondary agenda. Similarly, God has an agenda for every married couple, which is different from the first agenda. Single people are complete in their singlehood until God gives them a secondary agenda that requires marriage (Guidepost 1).

God finished creating Adam by giving him God's own living breath (and indirectly God's living breath is in Eve). With God's breath within them, their lives have a spiritual and relational dependence on God. When Adam and Eve lived dependently on God, they lived it out in the quality of oneness marked at the highest degree of closeness or unity, they approached God free of distrust of Him and free of inadequacy of His sufficiency for them; they were **Naked** and **Not Ashamed** (Guideposts 4 and 5, respectively).

When Adam and Eve interacted with God at that highest degree of oneness, being **Naked** and **Not Ashamed**, they also lived life in obedience to God's guidance and purpose for them. Conversely, when Adam and Eve stopped living in obedience to God's guidance and purpose, they instead chose to believe the guidance of the enemy of God, the deceiver Satan. From there, their relationship with God degraded to the lowest degree, void of closeness and unity; now they were **Hiding** and **Ashamed**, distrusted God and acted out of inadequacy. Similarly, Adam and Eve **hid** not only from **God** but also covered themselves from each other. Their disobedience to God became an obstruction between them as a couple, and they lost the closeness they once shared.

Adam and Eve's failure to steward and complete God's purpose for them as a couple (God's second agenda item for them) resulted in a demotion. God booted them from the garden, and they did not receive a celebration or honor. But fortunately, God does reward those who are obedient and faithful at the final **destination** as He describes in Revelation 2. We see that God promotes those who are faithful to steward the purpose God gives them. Likewise, those singles or married couples who are faithful to manage God's agenda for them will be **celebrated** (Guidepost 11) and **promoted** (Guidepost 12).

Guideposts Part I: Executing the Battle Plan

Based on the passages surrounding these six guideposts and our observation of being single for a combined 70 years, there are mainly two types of Christian singles. The first, Single Person A, is called to marriage and is successfully promoted into marriage with God's blessing of a spouse uniquely designed for them. Then, there is a second type, the Single Person B, who may or may not be called to eventual marriage, but they are frustrated in their singlehood and struggle at finding a relationship with God's unique spouse partner.

Single Person A has not listened to Satan tell lies about how incomplete of a creation he or she is as a single person. From our observations and experience, the biggest battle as a single is to feel inadequate as a person because of being single (a lie from the enemy). Successful singles haven't listened to or believed the enemy's lies and so stay **not ashamed** toward God about their singlehood. Instead, they stay actively obeying and doing God's calling for their lives with contentment in their singlehood. They don't allow the enemy's lie—"being single is a curse and a demotion"—to motivate them to disbelieve God. They remain open—**naked**—and continue to trust God, maintaining their closeness with Him.

Conversely, Single Person B, believes the lies of the enemy about singlehood. These singles believe they are second-rate, and they **hide** from God because they doubt His care for them as singles. They also believe they are inadequate to serve God as singles and thus have a lesser value to God. They may distrust God's good nature and loving intention towards them. These singles may genuinely love God, but they have major hindrances between them and God as they hold on to the misinformation from the enemy. They don't trust God and hold back from fulfilling God's primary agenda for them. They are in **Hiding** from being wholly involved in doing God's will. Also, they are not transparent with God, and they have allowed an impasse between themselves and God's work for their lives.

My bride, Elyssa, lived a single life akin to Single Person A. As the groom, I experienced a season of life like that of Single Person B. I had misgivings about God and the way He was managing my life. I dealt with the **shame** of feeling inadequate in God's view of me. This distrust foiled my full trust and closeness (**nakedness**) with God. I tried to **hide** my distrust and shame and further foiled my closeness with God by choosing my own initiatives to correct my singlehood. I cover this story in detail in Chapter 11 and in passing in Chapter 7.

Guidepost Part One Warning

Whether married or single, the enemy indirectly or explicitly challenges God's view of our completeness. The enemy twists people's comments and society's messages about what makes a single person or a marriage complete. Adam and Eve believed the enemy's lie that they were incomplete without having the extra knowledge that the forbidden tree held. Unfortunately, *no lie of the enemy is ever harmless. Nor are the enemy's ideas real alternatives to God's perfect wisdom.* In the end, all the enemy's lies accomplished was misguiding Adam and Eve to forfeit the celebration and promotion God would have had for them if they had properly stewarded His calling.

Guidepost Part One Activity 1:

- 9.1.1. What lies is the enemy trying to sell you about your singlehood or marriage?

___

- 9.1.2. How are you going to shatter those lies?

___

Guideposts Part One Celebration

Believing the enemy's lie about what makes us complete results in our demotion thus holding back from our calling. Fortunately, when we rebuke the enemy for his lies and believe God's purpose and truth for us, we get the immediate help of staying in the ideal **naked** and **not ashamed** state for which we were created. We then live in intimate closeness with God, ever trusting Him and avoiding hindrances to obeying Him. The good news is that once we change *our* perspective back to God's original perspective of us and for us, then we can pass through all the guideposts successfully, resulting in our celebration, promotion and fulfilling of our calling.

The Single Person B who transforms into the Single Person A gets to celebrate the promotion of receiving honor from God and more blessings than at first.

Elyssa was a honeymoon living single. She lived an exemplary life committed to God, and among many things she did "as unto the Lord," one of them was living a life of purity. Remaining a virgin for all of her thirty-two years and not kissing a man until her wedding day was a rare commitment to God. (Even though we believe it doesn't have to be rare to be a virgin.) She honored her body and lived a life of purity.

She was promoted from the single life into marriage in an extraordinary way. Namely, the day of the wedding, one of the most important things

God told her to do was to pass on the gift of purity to someone else. God told her to take time out of the busyness of that day and specifically reach out to a particular friend who was single. She prayed over her to receive special grace for maintaining her singlehood with purity. Elyssa is one example of someone who, though eventually called to be married, she lived life as a single person shining for God. Though we believe marriage is God's completion of creation, we are not saying that single people are incapable of equally stewarding God's purposes or bringing pleasure to the Lord with their lives surrendered to Him. Not only did Elyssa pass on her commitment to purity to that person on our wedding day, over the years leading up to our wedding, many others have profited from Elyssa's praying and interceding to God on their behalf to have restoration and perseverance in their purity.

Guideposts Part II: The Battle Plan's Offensive Weapons

The earlier discussion about these guideposts laid out how the **enemy's** primary attack strategy (Guidepost 6) is to create **shame** (Guidepost 5) in our core being. The enemy favors and masters injecting lies and deviations from God's truth to tempt whosoever among us would listen and believe we are incomplete people even though God has completed us in Himself. Or the second lie he favors is to suggest God is a malicious and a stingy Father and Creator God. It is important to know our enemy's main approach to tempting and attacking us. But it is even more important to know how to get on the offensive in the battle against the enemy.

In the battle for our hearts that continues since the beginning, we urgently need concrete solutions to stay on the offensive, whether as singles or married couples. A real, concrete solution makes our route more predictable as we travel to our final destination. Fortunately, in **Guidepost 7, Jesus has rewritten the manual on life, purpose, and marriage.** He fulfills two purposes for us. First, He provides an on-demand teaching manual for singlehood and marriage through His Holy Spirit. Second, Jesus's life functions as an example for how we can live vibrantly as singles and married couples. Ephesians tells us that Adam and Eve were supposed to fulfill their marriage purpose from God by **having faith in God** (Guidepost 9). They also were to act with obedience to their Father, a mark of **sonship or discipleship** (Guidepost 10), rather than disobedience and faithlessness in choosing the contradictory lie of the enemy.

Guideposts Part II: Executing the Battle Plan

From our observation of a combined seventy years of being single and as bystanders, many marriages are being severely attacked by the enemy. My bride and I were **on guard** (Guidepost 6) against the enemy as we entered our marriage. As soon as I heard of the master marriage counselor Jesus (Guidepost 7) with His excellent success rate, then my bride and I were determined to live by everything He was providing (the power of agape love, Guidepost 8, through the Holy Spirit) and teaching (the rewritten manual for a husband and wife, Guidepost 7).

My bride and I enrolled in the course Jesus was teaching (Guidepost 7) and decided we were going to do marriage by the book. Just like there was a Single Person A and B, we realized there was Married Person A and Married Person B. Married Person A believes God's voice and runs toward God and confronts the enemy's lies. We would invest only in activities of the Married Person A from the start of our marriage and forward.

The ceremony ended and off we went to the honeymoon. But what changed? We now had a license for intimacy. True. But something much, much greater than that also happened. It was startling how clearly reality had changed for us. We now had a newfound set of choices, just as Adam and Eve had choices. They had a choice to listen to and obey the guidance of God to tend and protect the garden or to reject God and listen to and obey the other voices that contradicted God. Because the enemy from the original garden is still present today (the already defeated devil that is the only source of those contradictory voices), we also had two opposite choices.

God's guidance and invitation to live out our new calling was always the higher, more glorious choice. The enemy always offered us the lower and convenience-based options. But the enemy shouted out his choices the loudest, trying to overpower God's guidance and invitation to us. What is striking is how absurd the enemy's plans are compared to God's plans. In the earlier chapter, Elyssa listed the choices she had to make after the wedding. Below are the three choices I (Wladimir) had to make.

Lesson 1 from Guidepost 7: As a husband, do I really have a role or duty to extend or sacrifice for her?

I woke up in the middle of our first night together and noticed the bed sheets were no longer covering Elyssa. We had very slippery silk sheets, and they were hard to keep aligned on the bed. It took extra effort to untangle and make the sheets cover us both. I had a choice: Do I take the extra effort to make sure she is covered with the sheets even though I am tired from our long wedding day? Do I do it out of some duty, a greater calling? Or is my own convenience more important? The enemy offered his own common but inferior rationale: "You've got her now; you don't have to overextend yourself any further. You can relax. Don't set too high a precedence because it will cost you. She is tough; she doesn't expect to be sacrificed for. She can live without it." In the end, I chose yes to God's invitation to make the sacrifice for Elyssa that night because I love her and I am her protector and God will always give me (or the agape-powered husband) adequate strength for the challenges I face if I live dependently on Him and trust in His design.

Lesson 2 from Guidepost 7: As a husband, do I have to earn the spiritual or marital leadership? Or is it a position that God equips me for, and I will succeed in based on my dependence on him?

My bride and I are both 6'1" tall. (We can each be shorter or taller depending on who used the back-roller most recently or who stretches out his/her back most often!) More importantly, my bride has been actively leading people and cultivating her leadership abilities through her job over the last seven years. The enemy gave me the option to immediately stand-down and let her lead our spiritual and marital relationship since I haven't actively been in leadership or cultivating my own leadership abilities. Though I am a leader, I am not as polished as is my bride. However, the Lord affirmed me, "You are the leader in this marriage because I have called you to this role, not based on your business leadership expertise."

I said, "Yes, Lord, I will trust your guidance because you have a blueprint for marriage that cannot fail."

The Lord said, "I haven't called you to outsmart or outwit your wife to win the leadership role in your marriage. My marriage design is not based on a balance of power, money, or anything else. Instead, it is based on how I, the Lord, ordained the two to become one flesh." I was thankful for God's guidance and encouragement. Also, I was thankful that my bride didn't contest my leadership but lovingly became like the bride of Christ to me, humbly living out the wedding vows she uttered to me.

Lessons from Guideposts 1 - 3: Should we spend our honeymoon fully learning about and loving each other? Or enjoying the resort and tourist amenities and connecting with the outside world through social media?

Temptation three was another absurd choice. Here I was on my honeymoon with my virgin bride, and I had a choice. I could allocate time to visit all the "must-see" sites and activities highlighted in our Cancun tour guide, or I could prioritize spending time alone with my bride because we had waited to be one and were finally made one. It seems absurd now, but in the first few days of our honeymoon, the temptation was strong to make the wrong choice. The enemy pressed in and said, "Hey, your spouse packed a lot of bathing suits; that means you need to spend a lot of time at the swimming pool. And people are going to ask you how Cancun was and about the resort where you stayed. They will want to see a tan line since you were in a tropical climate." Conversely, God's voice was clear, "You are to pay 100 percent attention to each other and zero percent attention to anything else.

You were made to complete each another. You cannot be too consumed or too drunk with her love. You cannot get too close or intimate with each other. You are one with each other; so, prioritize enjoying this oneness and marriage design I made."

After getting such a loving command and affirmation from the Lord, we dug in our heels. We resisted the go-be-a-tourist temptation that was presented to us. Instead, we built a love hut or a honeymoon end-of-the-world bunker, where all we needed was each other, a Bible, our devotional reading material, water, food, fresh towels, and sheets.

Lastly and interestingly, becoming a husband was fun. I didn't have to have earlier experience as a husband to succeed. Instead, God was giving me the just-in-time affirmation and guidance I needed to be an expert husband to my bride. My bride was similarly being an expert wife to me. We were learning to be expert spouses to each other because we were submitting to God's leadership (Guidepost 10, discipleship) about marriage and relying on him for the resources (Guidepost 7) we needed to succeed.

Guidepost 8: How Powerful is Agape love?

Thirteen days before Valentine's Day, I got a prompting that I was suppose to "build" a bouquet for Elyssa by purchasing and delivering to her a rose a day for twelve days leading up to Valentine's Day. Sounds like a sweet romantic gesture, right? Drive to the florist, pick up a rose, and deliver it to her at her office. Here's the catch: the prompting did not say to drive. It said, "Run! You start tomorrow." Like literally run, run across town to the florist, buy a rose, run it to her wherever she was (which most days was her office), tell her I love her, and then run home. Really?

Strange as it sounded, I followed that prompting, and here is what agape love overcame as I was building Elyssa her bouquet.

Agape Love in Action

Dearest Bride Elyssa, twelve days before Valentine's Day, I set out to build you a Valentine's Bouquet of a dozen roses, running each day to the florist and personally handpicking one rose and then delivering it to you, even though I hadn't been regularly running and I hadn't even calculated the distance.

Day One. *Tuesday, February 3, was the first day after the decision; it was rainy and cold. I waited and hoped the rain would go away, but it didn't stop. It just kept raining and raining. I contemplated, "Did I really make this commitment to run and pick up flowers each day until Valentine's Day and tell her I love her? How hard could it be to run in the rain and cold?" Well, the rain was not letting up, and the business day was coming close to an end.*

I set out running, and the coldness settling into my body said, "What are you doing? The honeymoon time away was over a month and a half ago. You don't have to act like you are still in the honeymoon phase. You will be fine to just buy a bouquet all at once on Valentine's Day."

I responded, 'No, no, no. I haven't left the honeymoon. Our marriage is still in the honeymoon phase, even though it's been weeks. I love you, Elyssa, and I am coming to you to tell you so."

Day Two. *Wednesday, February 4, the weather was decent, but I didn't know which roads had safe sidewalks. I felt a little afraid while running on stretches of roads that didn't have sidewalks.*

Those cars coming nearby said, "You don't have to do this. You might get hit." They asked me, "Do you love her that much? What would you do if you got hit? Are you going to run across the bridge without the sidewalks?"

The water beneath the bridge asked me, "What if you tripped and fell off the bridge, do you love you her?"

I said back, "I know I don't have to do this, but I love her. I love her. I love you sweetheart. I am coming to tell you; I am coming to be with you. Shut up, cars and water underneath the bridge. If I get hit, I will make arrangement to get a rose delivered to her each day by my in-laws or friends in town because I love her. If I get hit, I will ask the doctor for special permission and make special arrangements."

9 HONEYMOON LIVING

Day Three. *Thursday, February 5,* the cars were nicer. I hadn't run three days in row in probably a decade.

My body asked me, "Do you love her? No one knows you made a commitment to build her a twelve-day bouquet. It is okay to rest today. Just get one extra rose on Valentine's Day, and it will still be a dozen."

My knees asked, "Do you really love her? Are you really on a honeymoon right now? Really, is marital love that powerful to make you a runner?"

I said, "Yes, Yes, I love you Elyssa. With all my heart and now with my body, I say I love you. I will reach you soon and tell you I love you!"

Day Four. *Friday, February 6,* my body was not nicer. I hadn't run four days in a row probably in all my thirty-eight years of existance. Also, now the not-for-no-reason nickname for the area we live, "Hill Country," was now starting to speak to me.

My body and the hills were talking to me, "Hey there, do you love her? Are you still on a honeymoon?"

I said "Yes, Yes."

They asked, "Are you going to prove it? Your body is fragile, you know, and you've never done this before."

I said, "I will make it. Love will carry me and is carrying me now. I love you, Elyssa. I am coming to say, 'I love you, I love you, I love you.' You have completed me, and I will make it to you because the hills and my body can't stop me. In fact, I think I am going to start to think about something else. Oh, like all the ways I can be praying for you right now. Please help her, Lord, bless her, Lord, and thank you, Lord, for her. Thank you for making her mighty. In Jesus' name, amen!"

Day Five. *Saturday, February 7,* my body was nicer to me. It was a hot day. I needed to keep the secret commitment going. I needed the perfect alibi to leave the house for my run-for-a-rose and yet remain undetected while I went. My possible alibi was that we had a broken water filter at home and desperately needed a gallon of filtered water. While she was lying in bed, I made a getaway. It was a hot day, and I forgot my water bottle at home.

As I ran, growing hotter by the mile, the sunshine unmistakably asked, "Do you love her?"

Both my sweat and the sweat-splashed pavement asked me, "Do you love her? Is love able to overtake you and transform you that much? Can marriage really give you superhuman strength?"

I answered the sun, sweat, and pavement, "Yes, I love her, and love is divine and has transformed me." While getting the rose, I started to see an issue with running back nearly two miles with the much-needed gallon of filtered water.

My body thought, "Surely I could run to deliver the rose and then return by car to pick up the gallon of water."

But I said, "She will be expecting the water when I get there." Hence, I ran back home with the gallon, and rose in hand.

The gallon, the sun, the sweat, the pavement, and the thirst jumped on me and said, "Are you sorry now that you love her?"

I said, "I am not sorry that I love her. I love you, Elyssa. Our marriage love is divine. I love you, I will see you soon, and I will raise my glass with you to love!"

Day Six. Sunday, February 8, everything was nice to me. My body ached, but cheered, "Way to go on loving her."

It was about 81 degrees, and the sun said, "Way to go, love really is divine, enjoy the power of love."

The sweat and pavement said, "Kudos on the love and marriage."

The cars said, "You are always safe and protected under divine love. Keep going."

The rose in my hand cheered for Elyssa and our divine love, while the air, my sweat, and sun splashed on it. Even my bright orange neon jacket cheered me on.

Days Seven through Nine. Monday, Tuesday, Wednesday, February 9-11, all cheered.

Day Ten. *Thursday, February 12, and Valentine's Day was just two days away. So close but still far enough, since nothing but twelve daily delivered roses would do.* I sprained my right ankle on the sidewalk.

My right ankle, pained yet rooting for me, suggested, "We can walk or drive the car to deliver the roses for the remaining two days if I don't heal."

I reached out to God and pleaded, "In the name of God and because of divine love, please miraculously heal my ankle and let me not have an injury. Thank you. In the name of Jesus, amen." I kept running, and then noticed no pain or sprain or any ache in any part of my body.

The healing cheered me, "You love her!"

The ankle cheered, "You love her!"

Day Eleven. *Friday, February, 13, I was excited. So close to the finish line!*

Day Twelve. *Saturday, February 14, the day is here. Happy Valentine's Day is here!* I had made it to the twelfth day, but the first five roses of the bouquet had wilted.

Those five roses said, "Hey, we request to be replaced with five fresh and proper roses to be joined to the twelfth rose." I set out again to get the twelfth rose, plus five replacements.

The road, my feet, the sunshine, and Valentine's Day all celebrated with me, "The finish line is here. You have faced every obstacle and overcome; you have shown extravagant love, and victory is here!"

I raced home to complete the bouquet and ran into the house with the final roses to my beautiful bride. "Elyssa, I love you more today than I loved you yesterday. I want to love you more. Tomorrow I will love you even more than I love you today by the help of the Holy Spirit. Love and marriage is amazing! I love you, Sweetest Heart Pie!"

Guidepost Part Two Warning

I can tell you from running the equivalent of two marathons to build Elyssa a bouquet that everything in me plus more was needed to complete the task.

Even power far beyond my own strength was required. That Valentine's Day was a triumphant victory. It was a demonstration of agape love and a celebration of the power of a honeymoon marriage. It was a direct correlation to what the Lord had been teaching me in 1 Corinthians 13 (Guidepost 8), which we covered in Chapter 6 in more detail.

Love is meant to possess you. You cannot have control over it; it must have control over you. When it does, agape love will make you brave, and the person receiving the love can become brave as they accept the love fully. Conversely, the love in life or marriage that isn't agape love equates to the love that may produce results but are not adequate to be worthy of celebration in eternity. Even worse, it gets a failing grade in the final promotion or demotion evaluation in the Scriptures in Revelation two (Guidepost 11). Fortunately, with agape love, you will fight past your limits and soar. With agape love, you demonstrate the total abandonment of Christ's love poured out. Agape love inspires. Agape love changes things. Wedding vows are possible to be fulfilled with agape love. Live from that place—radically abandoned and empowered by God's strength and His love.

Guidepost Part Two Activity 1:

- 9.2.1. When was the last time you let agape love overtake you and bring you to new heights in your love for your spouse, and what did you overcome?

_____

_____

- 9.2.2. Can your love go to the next level?

_____

- 9.2.3. What is that next level for you and how are you going to demonstrate that love with magnitude?

_____

Guidepost Part Two Celebration

Honeymoon living produces a life full of opportunities for spontaneous and frequent celebrations. Marriage can be lived from a defensive stance, bobbing and weaving against the lies the enemy is throwing at us. Or we can be on the offensive, constantly enjoying God's blessings of marriage and letting it produce joyous celebrations interspersed throughout our days. Following Jesus's teaching allows for much celebration, and staying on the offensive makes us perpetual champions of marriage.

Below is a short guide to becoming celebration experts in your marriage:

- Become the biggest flirt to your spouse. If your spouse isn't mystified at how you managed to sneak in a flirt with him or her during some regular daily exchange or activity, then you are not the biggest flirt to your spouse.

- Pen dates on your calendar. You can both trade off the responsibility. *Avoid one spouse always having to plan and carry out the dates.* Instead, put many date activities on your calendar. Try adding two bi-weekly events into your schedule: one for even weekends, the other for odd weekends. Each spouse could "own" the weekend date festivities for that week. For example, the spouse responsible for the weekend could bring breakfast to bed, prep the meals, select the movie or outing, etc.

- Celebrate each other over the top because you are joined to be one. You are each other's greatest necessity and gift. Whether you have anything else on earth, God has made you to be completed only by your spouse and vice-versa. No other substitutes can complete you in this way—no activities, no amount of money, no fame, nothing.

Some celebration ideas:

- Why not have anniversaries every month instead of every year? In our marriage, we added two bi-monthly events into our calendar schedule: one for even months, the other for odd months. We each "own" the odd or even month and anniversary celebration for that month. One of us will intentionally do a little something special during the week of our monthly anniversary: write something, cook something, pray something, or find something that God is doing. Then, we take a little time together to celebrate each other and to remember that God has brought us together for His purpose.

- Why not over-indulge on your wedding pictures and have them plastered all around your living space? Or put photos from your honeymoon or a vacation in a digital picture frame to relive the celebration memories. For us, we created a "Honeymoon Just Married" and a "Honeymoon for Life" car window decals to celebrate continuously our forever "Just Married" status and our honeymoon mode "For Life."

Rewards of Becoming Marriage Celebration Experts

One unintended consequence of becoming marriage celebration experts is that other people also begin to celebrate your marriage. Below are some positive signs from others about how successfully you are celebrating your marriage:

- You will have a married life that is appreciated by others.

- You will mystify your spouse by how kind you act toward each other. They will be baffled by the loving acts you have done for them without looking for something in return.

- You will have a married life that inspires others, your community, and especially your children (if you are parents).

- Something about your relationship toward each other, whether it is your loving-kindness, harmony, unity, or connectedness will mystify your community. And people will appreciate your loving relationship and the beauty that shines from it.

- Best of all, you will live without regrets and experience God's promotion from your obedience to living and loving at His standard of love (Guidepost 12).

We are cheering for you and believe your life as a single or as a married person can shine. The Heavenly Father will reward your obedience to steward carefully His call on your life.

We have covered only the tip of the iceberg in this chapter. Much more will be added in future books and media in this series. For now, in the next two chapters, we offer practical and specific actions you can take to redirect your married or single life toward honeymoon living. Or, if you feel that darkness has begun to overtake your singlehood or marriage, it is time to shine God's light into the night and unleash a revolution in your life.

10 HONEYMOON REVOLUTION: SINGLES ROADMAP

In this chapter, we cover the most urgent information to help single adults (whether or not currently dating) to truly succeed while they are not married. The single can stay strong and avoid a myriad of dating relationship experiences marked by pain, confusion, and premature, unfulfilling intimacy.

We believe singlehood can be beautifully lived out with confidence and a revolutionary spirit. However, singles need the right information to live their singlehood successfully! This chapter is in an interactive workbook format so the single person can gain the maximum benefit. Hence, we will frequently prompt the reader to pause and answer questions, observe, or perform an exercise.

Your Singles & Dating Revolution Roadmap Activities

The rest of this chapter is in an interactive workbook format.

How? We will frequently prompt the readers to pause and observe, answer questions, brainstorm, or invite them to check out external tools to get further help. *Also note: when an activity references scripture passages, we encourage you to follow along in The Scriptures, using your Bible or one online. In most activities, we will use The Amplified® Bible Translation, (AMP). When Wladimir or Elyssa is making a summary observation of a scripture passage, it will be marked "WEJ-Paraphrase."*

Why? **FIRST**, so you the reader can gain the maximum benefit through participation. **SECOND**, to permit later interactive activities to be-added-on, and accelerate the benefits you gain from the material. **THIRD**, to permit a bridge to have later live interaction with authors and teams dedicated to championing your success in singlehood, marriage, and love by God's design. **FORTH**, as you work through the activities below, you may find yourself wanting to go deeper and explore more.

Additional tools and support at:

www.ThePowerOfAHoneymoon.com/phmtools

Get Your Preliminary Baseline

Activity 10.1

Brainstorm: If you are a Christian single (with a desire to marry), what is the best motivation and focus to have while you are not married?

_____

_____

_____

To go deeper on section 10.1

Visit *www.*ThePowerOfAHoneymoon.com/phmtools

Here is a little bit of what we discovered as we brainstormed the question above.

Elyssa, "I had a pretty clear understanding of the blessings of living out God's plan for my life while I was single. I was *current moment* focused and *future* focused, meaning that I worked hard to make sure that the way that I lived life in my current state of singlehood was honoring to my future spouse. I was also positively focused and motivated for my future wedding, honeymoon, and life with my spouse. I did not wait for that day passively, but with expectancy and preparation, believing that my future husband and our life together would be worth the wait."

Wladimir, "As the groom: As soon as I figured out God was calling me to eventually marry, I wished I had had the same goal as Elyssa. I wish during my singlehood that I had been positively motivated by my future honeymoon night and the special time with my spouse who would be a person that was worth the wait. This is the clarity I wish I had while I was single."

Activity 10.2

Brainstorm:

- 10.2.1. What are your convictions about pre-marital sex?

　_____
　_____

- 10.2.2. How important to you is it that you and your future spouse enter marriage completely sexually present and free from all attachments from past sexual experiences?

　_____
　_____

- 10.2.3. What would make your future honeymoon night and your future spouse *worth the wait* for you?

　_____
　_____

If you are bold, you can share with us your answers. *(Join us online and tell us in the go deeper section 10.2 activities.)*

To go deeper on section 10.2

Visit *www.*ThePowerOfAHoneymoon.com/phmtools

Activity 10.3

Brainstorm three to six phrases in the six blank lines below before proceeding. To help focus the brainstorm, please start your sentences beginning with things like, "I wish my future husband / wife / wedding / guest / honeymoon…"

Examples: I wish my future husband is hot and hunky. I wish my future wedding day extravagantly shows off the goodness of God.

_____
_____
_____
_____
_____
_____

To go deeper on section 10.3
Visit *www.*ThePowerOfAHoneymoon.com/phmtools

Here are a few questions to think through as you process your thoughts and work through the exercises in this chapter

1. How important is it to me to be fully connected to my spouse going into our wedding day?
2. What would make the honeymoon night extremely special and romantic and allow me to be fully connected to my spouse?
3. What is sexual freedom? Is there a correlation between the passion, excitement and freedom on our honeymoon night with how sexually free we are entering marriage?
4. Do I need to be freed from any sexual history in the past or from any trauma that may have occurred in the past (especially spiritual, sexual, emotional, or physical abuse)?
5. If there are sexual experiences in the past, how should I undo the attachment to those past experiences?

6. What would make the next day after the honeymoon night, and the beginning of our life together special?

Activity 10.4

- 10.4.1. What are your highest ideals?
  _____
  _____
  _____

- 10.4.2. Summarize your highest ideals by writing three observations that emerged as you worked through the exercises above.
  _____
  _____
  _____

To go deeper on section 10.4
*Visit www.*ThePowerOfAHoneymoon.com/phmtools

Activity 10.5

If you had three special wishes:

1. One wish for your wedding day.

2. One wish for your wedding night.

3. One wish for your life after your wedding.

What would your wishes be?

1. _____

2. _____

3. _____

Part 1: You Are Single and Not a Virgin (Nor a Rededicated Virgin)

Culture promotes many messages about sexuality, but there is no replacement for God's design of sex. God is not a cosmic killjoy, He is not anti-sex, and in fact starting with Adam and Eve in the creation story and continuing through the Bible sex is encouraged and celebrated. However, God does have some guidelines in His blueprint for sexuality. Simply summed up His blueprint on sex is Honor God (by living according to His design for sex). Honor ourselves (by not giving ourselves to others sexually prior to marriage). Honor our future spouse's body (by stewarding correctly the gift God is giving us). Once married, it is game on!

Reflecting back on the groom's experience from the day of our wedding might be beneficial to singles reading now. Here goes:

The day of my wedding, I was a wreck. I was happy that I was about to marry God's Plan A for my life and that God gave me a woman He had fashioned *just for me*—to be my helpmate. However, I had nineteen years of being a Christian scrolling through my memory, and for a handful of those years, I did not live with an undivided heart that trusted God for His provision of my needs. As I cried tears of thankfulness to God for being faithful to me, I also shed tears of sadness. Since I first started following Christ in 1994, I hadn't always stayed focused on God. I had allowed myself to backslide into premarital sexual sins.

That part of my story is not, *I repeat*, is *not* God's blueprint for thriving in singlehood. It was not my self-righteousness or my strong self-will that I was grieving about, though I knew they were sins, too. But on my wedding day, standing before my virgin bride, I wished I had withstood the sexual temptations. Instead, I grieved those nineteen years of being single, being a Christ-follower, not always living with sexual purity, and honoring God, my future spouse and myself fully.

Activity 10.6

- 10.6.1. If you are not married and are sexually active or have been sexually active and you call yourself a Christian, are you ready to stop living with this contradiction? Check "Yes" or "No".

Yes _____ / No _____,
If No, Why?
_____
_____

To go deeper on section 10.6
   Visit www.ThePowerOfAHoneymoon.com/phmtools

I knew that this period of my life, with the sexual compromise and detour, brought dishonor to God's reputation. Similarly, any believer that would make the same kind of sexual compromise and detour does bring shame to God's reputation. I am sad about the dishonor I brought to God's reputation. And this compromise, had I not eventually stopped, also would have robbed me of being able to properly steward my virgin bride. As she and I talked about this subject, she indicated her readiness to abort our relationship if I had attempted to cross any lines sexually.

For multimedia companion on this section #10.6.2
   Visit www.ThePowerOfAHoneymoon.com/phmmedia

> **Critical Warning**
>
> Your wedding day can be a day full of praise and no sorrows. Yes, praises can produce tears, but those tears are sweet rather than sorrowful. Aim for tears of joy and praises to God for your wedding day, when God writes your "Adam and Eve" wedding story.
>
> *For multimedia companion on this section #10.6.3*
>   Visit www.ThePowerOfAHoneymoon.com/phmmedia

How do you resist the detours of premarital sex? Love for God as your *first love* is the unrivaled motivation that will keep the single person focused and most equipped to enter into marriage successfully, without compromise.

Cultivate your first love for God and let Him cultivate and use His gifts in you.

Without having the clear aim of cultivating my first love for God and letting Him cultivate His gifts in me, I found myself in sin management mode. That is, I was focused on how to avoid having sex before marriage or constantly looking toward to the future when I *could* have sex. Both are weak motivations and poor sources for contentment. They leave you sexually frustrated rather than entering into your wedding night and marriage ready to roar like a lion that is protecting his territory or like a lioness who wants to take down prey and build the territory with her lion king.

Being sexually frustrated is a poor signal that you are ready for marriage. Yes, sex with your spouse is glorious, but marriage is much more than permission to have sex. Therefore, when you are single with a desire to marry, plan to have a revolutionary single life that prepares you to excel far beyond being sexually knowledgeable on your wedding night. *There is a lie and temptation thrown at us by the common marriage enemy and by society. It says, "Hey, you should be knowledgeable of your future spouse's sexual abilities."* That trap leads you to bondage. The roadmap for you to reach a honeymoon marriage begins with knowing who you are and were created to be, growing in scripture, spiritual disciplines, and life skills (financial management, relational-people skills), and getting involved in using your giftedness for God.

Part 2: Slay the Dragon(s) of Your Sexual Past

Let's Start with God's Blueprint about SEX: 1 Corinthians 6:16-20

AMP (1 Cor. 6:16)

> Or do you not know and realize that when a man joins himself to a prostitute, he becomes one body with her? The two, it is written, shall become one flesh.

WEJ-Paraphrase (1 Cor. 6:16)

Any sex between two people is a reenactment of creation and the first marriage story.

AMP (1 Cor. 6:17)

But the person who is united to the Lord becomes one spirit with Him.

WEJ-Paraphrase (1 Cor. 6:17)

This is mystical. However, a Christian receives an indwelling closeness to Jesus that is comparable to the oneness and closeness of a married couple.

AMP (1 Cor. 6:18)

Shun immorality and all sexual looseness [flee from impurity in thought, word, or deed]. Any other sin which a man commits is one outside the body, but he who commits sexual immorality sins against his own body.

WEJ-Paraphrase (1 Cor. 6:18)

In light of the indwelling closeness that exists in marriage, sexual sin should be abhorred in all forms.

AMP (1 Cor. 6:19)

Do you not know that your body is the temple (the very sanctuary) of the Holy Spirit Who lives within you, Whom you have received [as a Gift] from God? You are not your own,

WEJ-Paraphrase (1 Cor. 6:19)

Not to mention, a Christian's physical body is a claimed and set apart item; therefore, it deserves careful treatment. Sex or joining with a person who is not your spouse is not a careful use of the body.

AMP (1 Cor. 6:20)

You were bought with a price [purchased with a preciousness and paid for, made His own]. So then, honor God and bring glory to Him in your body.

WEJ-Paraphrase (1 Cor. 6:20)

A Christian is bought or redeemed at both a spiritual and physical level, hence it matters how we steward our body in view of God's graciousness towards us.

※ ※ ※

Prerequisites to True Singlehood

When I recommitted to Christ in my mind and heart that I would obey Him and no longer have sex before marriage, I still needed to undo the previous joining I did with past girlfriends (that is, I needed deliverance from the strong "oneness" bond that always happens between any two people in a sexual relationship). I undid ties and severed the attachments of connectedness to my premarital sexual past. Without this, there would have been a lingering pull at my soul.

Critical Warning

As a single who is not a virgin, if you do not receive personal deliverance from the previous sexual incidents, you will experience a nagging connection and a lack of closure with your past. Ensure this gets undone immediately, because if left undone, your past will continue to have influence over your present thoughts.

Revolution In Action - 1

This is how I cut the spiritual ties to my past girlfriends. I prayed and invited the Holy Spirit and the power of God to come bring freedom from my sexual past. I acknowledged that receiving freedom from my sexual past was God's desire for me. I then said the name of the woman I had had sex with, and then I asked God to reverse the sexual ties and attachments that I had to that person. I stated I forgave her. Then, over the next forty-eight hours, I felt a complete break from that spiritual "oneness" I had had with that other person. It was gone forever.

Your Revolution In Action – 1 part 1, If Applicable Don't Wait Another Minute

To experience this freedom for yourself, pray through these steps:

1) Invite the Holy Spirit and the power of God to come bring freedom from your sexual past and start agreeing with and accepting the truth of scripture, that sexual joining with another person outside of marriage is not God's standard.

2) Next, agree that the past sexual attachments are holding you in bondage and are against God's plan for you.

3) Say the person's name that you are sexually tied to or had a sexual encounter with and ask God to reverse and free you from those ties and then, forgive that person.

4) Finally, move forward and look for discernible liberty and freedom regarding any past emotional or physical attachment that once existed.

Critical Warning

Most people don't know the real pain and deficient that is done to themselves and the other person by engaging in premarital sex acts. Most often, the other person was not looking to maliciously hurt you and you were not looking to maliciously hurt them, their wedding night and their marriage, nor were you looking to sabotage yourself and hurt your future spouse, or degrade your wedding night and your marriage. Forgiving yourself and forgiving the other person is critical. It helps set you free and helps set them free and lets you move unhindered toward God and your future.

Ask God to show you each person that you are improperly tied to from your past and for each of those people do the above process. This sort of personal removing of ties and attachments is not limited to just sexual encounters, you can work through the same process if you have improper emotional attachments with another person or have other areas of your life that you feel powerless to fight against. This sort of prayer is taught in the Bible. Further information, help, resources and training is available.

To go deeper on this section 10, #PersonalDeliverance
*Visit www.*ThePowerOfAHoneymoon.com/phmtools

* * *

If you choose not to undo the past ties, on your wedding night and in your marriage, you and your spouse will feel the negative impact of the ties from your past. They will negatively diminish the important closeness you should feel only with your spouse. When married, we are called to have no interference from past sexual relationships with others. With those experiences no longer lingering or never existing, then you and your spouse get to experience an amazing connectedness.

Your Revolution In Action – 1 part 2

Keep your spiritual disciplines intact

Scripture reading, prayer, fasting, regularly using God's gifts both directly and indirectly in God's work keep you strong. Since the enemy will not tire at suggesting the lie, you are inadequate as a single. However, you will unnecessarily struggle to fight the enemy's lies about your completion in God, if you spend insufficient daily time actively growing in your knowledge of, experience with, and dependence on God. Give Him the opportunity to steadily eradicate doubts about His active care for you. Also let Him affirm to you His ability to sustain you and cause you to thrive during any length of your singlehood. Your adequacy or completion during your singlehood is always in your dependence on God alone, never anything else.

Example of spiritual disciplines in action

- Reading the Bible in 90-days, or 1-year

- Journaling your prayers

- Going on spiritual retreats

Just to list a few rigorous regular actions to keep intact so your strength, knowledge, awareness and dependence on God grows brighter.

Part 3: You Are Now Dating

Our dating journey began online at eHarmony.com and was built despite the distance of miles between us. Elyssa lived near San Antonio, Texas and I lived in Chicago, Illinois. While we were dating we met at unlikely locations around the country: in Baltimore, Maryland, for business training at "First Steps to Success," in Atlanta, Georgia, for business training at "Creating a Dynasty," the memorial site at the World Trade Center-Ground Zero, my grandmother's funeral in Long Island, New York, and in Orlando, Florida, at the talent training and scouting event, A.M.T.C. Summer Shine 2014.

For multimedia companion on this section 10, #NowDating
   Visit www.ThePowerOfAHoneymoon.com/phmmedia

This is the short list of our dating exploits. We trekked a remarkable path, had a fantastic wedding and honeymoon beginning, and now we lead an unusually confident, loving, grounded, inspirational marriage.

Many people ask us, "How did you two date so successfully?"

While dating, we cultivated an intimacy with the Lord that surpassed intimacy with each other. We tapped into God's immense spiritual power to do mighty work for the Lord while we were dating; we started to work on a book and curriculum about marriage. As singles before we even met each other, we both were immersed in doing God's work, such as exploring modeling, church pastoring, etc. That season of preparation and cultivating our gifts eventually helped shape how we would live as a married couple (joined to God's Plan A for each of us). Our focus in our singlehood and the fun and rewarding dating relationship we fostered caused us to grow in the knowledge of God's will for our married life together.

Revolution In Action - 2

For the success of our dating and marriage relationship, we urgently needed to break the typical modern rules about dating (also the standard rules about marriage).

Your Revolution In Action – 2

Observe: Begin to notice the things you do and the kind of person you are while you are dating. What are some of the roots that are being formed in your dating relationship that will lead to habits in your marriage? What actions are as second nature to you but void of spiritual freshness?

Act: Stop doing what comes naturally, especially if those things "appear" to be instinctual or common sense but are done without spiritual dependence on God.

Revolution In Action - 3

We started moving in the opposite direction of our comfort zone and supercharging the priority, we placed on nurturing our spiritual senses. Those choices gave us the guidance we needed to navigate our relationship. For example, while listening to Christian radio, we heard a useful statistic: married couples who pray or do devotions together at least four days a week report a remarkable marriage satisfaction and success rate of more than 90 percent.

From that discovery, while we were dating, we decided to prioritize doing devotions together and we also committed to holding each other accountable to each do our personal spiritual devotional quiet times at least four days a week. (The lesson here is that prioritizing spiritual growth opportunities allowed us to choose more spiritually nourishing practices, which increased our confidence and clarity about our future individually and together.)

Your Revolution In Action - 3

Fortunately, **we went the uncommon extra mile in our singlehood and dating.** *All* **the activities we did together counted positively for our future.** However, the spiritual activities—like doing marriage devotional readings together and ensuring we each had rigorous devotional daily lives made the key difference in our dating life and even now in our married life.

When you are dating or are single, know that you can nurture activities that will be counted positively toward your future ability to stand strong as a lifetime single or as a married person. Hence, choose your present activities with an eye to please God in a moment, and this will help your present and your future.

The above recommendation paves the way for the real, bold fun that occurs when your relationship is built on the firm foundation shown in the authentic blueprint. While Elyssa and I were dating, we had bold fun, traveling to wonderful places and sharing many exploits. During this time, we actually built the footing for our rock solid marriage because we were grounded on these critical principles.

Join us online for a few more ideas on spiritual activities for you as a dating couple.

To go deeper on this section 10, #RevolutionAction-3

*Visit www.*ThePowerOfAHoneymoon.com/phmtools

Part 4: You are Single and a Virgin (or a Rededicated Virgin)

Is keeping my virginity really worth it?

If I could tell you one thing, it would be this: it is worth the wait! There are so many temptations and messages fighting against your purity and virginity. Culture will attack you. At times you will feel like you are all alone. You may feel mocked. But let me tell you this: there is nothing in the world that beats triumphing in the "impossible." The odds may seem against you, but there is One (The Lord God) who is for you. Above any mockery you may receive, there is One who stands for you. God cheers for you. When you feel all alone, call on Him. He does not fail. When you feel like you can't go on, call on Him. He will carry you. You have a gift, and you were created for this moment. You have what it takes to conquer the temptations and loneliness.

I know for sure you will not regret setting a high bar and holding to it. If you are a virgin (and/or are committed to celibacy until marriage), know that is it worth every bit of the fight for you to get there.

I am married to the most amazing man! It would not have been possible for us to experience the wondrous dating adventure that we had and the beautiful marriage that we have now had I not pressed through many obstacles over the years. Between the two of us, we accumulated seventy years of singlehood—Wladimir was thirty-eight, and I was thirty-two when we got married. Seventy years is a long time, but it was worth the wait! It was worth saving myself for him. It was worth walking away from every opportunity that could have led me to compromise. It was worth every social engagement that I attended without a date. All the countless nights alone were worth it. Totally worth it.

Revolution In Action - 4

The Virgin Bride's story

Yes, I was a virgin on my wedding day. What's more, I actually had my first kiss at the altar when the preacher said, *"You may kiss your bride."* The triumph of that day was nothing short of glorious. I had reached the goal. I had honored God. I had set a standard, an example, and I had made it.

The following are things I did in my single years that really helped me prepare for my wedding day and marriage:

1. **Dream with God.** Have God-sized dreams for yourself, and put those dreams into action. The world will tell you to settle. Do not settle. Reach for what others think is impossible, and believe God in your journey.

2. **Create a God-Sized Dream List for who your future spouse will be.** It's okay to list physical preferences you have if you want to, but go deeper than that. Ask God what He would want for you, and create your future spouse list from what He reveals. What would you dream for? Put those dreams to paper.

Below is a list I created when I was dreaming with God about who my future spouse would be. It was written seven and a half years before I met my husband. When you read the list below, some of it may not make sense or may seem silly to you; that's okay. Have you ever seen a modern art piece where it looked like the artist threw random paint colors all over a canvas? That is kind of what this list is like. God and I hung out together, I grabbed a blank piece of paper, and together we threw "paint" all over the paper. The list below is the canvas of a dreaming with God session, it shows little pieces of God's heart and plans for me. I tried to capture what He was saying and what I was feeling in my spirit and put it into words on paper and at the same time I was processing and trying to document some very intimate things that were in my heart. Sometimes the deep things of the heart do not really seem to make sense on paper.

Elyssa's Future Dream Spouse List (written May 25, 2006)

> *He is a man after God's heart and lives out holiness. He is passionate, pure of heart, honest, worthy of me, a builder of the kingdom God. He has a business mind and is good at business. He has the heart of a soldier and the mind of a warrior. He is tall, dark, hot, and handsome. He is the "best- of-the-best," the one where all the girls*

say, "Dang, she got him. He's the best." He is my best friend and my passionate lover and has eyes for me only. My husband is someone I can build a dynasty with, someone who rocks the nations by the power of God, and we minister to the entire world together. He is incredible in dealing with finances. He has a billionaire mindset. (I had no idea what a "billionaire mindset" looked like, but I felt it in my spirit and wrote it down.) He is focused and someone who can strengthen me, lead me spiritually, be the head of the house, plus be the leader in our relationship. He is someone I can trust. He has a heart for kids, for the broken, poor, and enslaved. The heart of Christ is reflected in him. He is a father in the truest sense of the word. He is a kick butt guy, a man with strength (both physical and spiritual). He is a guy whom demons run from and someone who sets captives free by the power of Christ. He is sexy, gorgeous, gifted, has a father's heart, is a leader, a builder, a protector, musically gifted (or at least appreciates it), and athletic. He is my soul mate, God's perfect match for me. We are created for each other. He is humble and is someone I can be myself with. He appreciates me and gets my sense of humor. He hears from God and acts according to God's will. He is not afraid to get dirty (meaning he is not afraid to tackle tough things and go where others would run from). He is someone who is very attracted to me, who loves me and has eyes only for me (meaning he doesn't have a divided heart). He is someone I can call mine. Someone worth the wait! He is someone who prays for me and someone I can serve and serve with. He likes people and can handle the spotlight but doesn't have to be the focus all the time (meaning he is not distracted by the attention of others). He is truthful, someone I can trust my life with, is a good father, and is dedicated.

When I wrote that list, I looked at it and felt overwhelmed. It felt impossible. I thought, "If somebody else sees this, they will think I have a really inflated opinion of myself." I hadn't written it from a self-inflated heart, though. I wrote it as I dreamed with God.

Critical Warning

God's desires and dreams for your life are much bigger than your own, and they are much bigger than anything other people would tell you are possible.

Your Revolution In Action - 4

Your Turn. Find a piece of paper and let the world and all that is going on around you pause. Take the time to dream with God, and to ask Him about the person He has set aside for you, ask Him to help you to be vulnerable and help you put your dreams and His dreams onto paper. Do not limit what God speaks to you; throw the "paint" on the "canvas" together.

3. There is a process that must take place. When I looked at the above list, I realized something: I was nowhere near who I personally needed to be in order to be married to the man on that list. I needed to *become his dream girl.* If the man on my list were writing his own list for his dream bride, then I would need to be the woman that was on *his* list. I would need to be who he was looking for. When I read over the list, I wrote of who I wanted him to be, I knew that I did not need to look for that man. I needed to become the woman that would fit beside him. If I wanted him to "rock the nations, to live out holiness, to be passionate, to be a leader, to have a billionaire mindset, and to have eyes only for me," then *that is who I had to be.* I needed to live out holiness, I needed to be passionate, I needed to develop my mindset, and I needed to have eyes for him only. From that list, I set my course, not to go find him but to let God make me the woman he needed as his helpmate. Simply stated, I worked on myself to *become the list* above. (Well, *most* of the list, I obviously did not need to become the masculine specific things like, "Tall dark and handsome or a father figure, etcetera.)

4. Focus on being all that God has called you to be. After I looked at the list of who my future husband was and had decided that I was going to focus on whom I needed to be in order to stand next to him, I set out to become the list and become who God was calling me to be. But I also took the process a step further and I wrote down an additional list. A list of who I was committing to be as his future wife.

Revolution In Action - 5

Elyssa's List Of Who She Was Committing To Be As A Wife Someday (Written May 25, 2006)

> *I will be passionate, dedicated, and beloved. I will represent Christ and act worthy of the groom God has given me. I will be slow to anger, forgiving, and loving. I will be a Proverbs 31 woman and work to be the best wife that I can be to my husband. I will prioritize sex, keep it fresh and fun, and never lose my enthusiasm. I will not let life pull me down or keep me down. I will be confident in who I am; I will take the time to make myself beautiful for him. I will treat him like a rock star. I will always keep God first and grow in my relationship with God. I will explore new things and keep up my energy. I commit to the process of staying totally attracted to my spouse and do my part to grow his attraction to me. I will keep God the center of our relationship. I will be pure (body, mind, and soul). I will have eyes for him alone—always and forever. I will be a great lover and friend, true to him. I will fulfill his "dream girl" list. I will be sexy and hot for him, turn him on and fulfill his needs. I will honor, honor, and honor him.*

From the time I wrote my commitment list, I waited eight and a half more years for my "worth the wait spouse" and first kiss on my wedding day.

Your Revolution In Action - 5

Pray. Please pray for what should go on the list for the spouse of your dreams. And then pray for what should go on a list for which you are committing to be.

Store your lists somewhere safe. Like your jewelry box, a safety deposit box, in an online storage cloud, etc. I put mine in an important business binder I knew I would be careful not to lose.

Take the time to go through the process of creating your lists. It was such a triumphant moment when I read those lists to my husband. They are cornerstone documents of the miracles God made happen in our lives. Wladimir was amazed when I pulled those lists out and read them to him after we were married. He had become the man on that list, I had become his dream girl, and God had brought us together.

More Ways to Cultivate Your Journey to Your Spouse

Remember that your future spouse is a real person that God has created for you and you for them. They are as real as you are. He/she has a name, a face, a story, and emotions, just like you, just because you haven't married him/her yet does not make him/her any less real. As you journey with God, allow Him to give you His ideas of how to honor your spouse even while you wait for him/her. You can do little things for your spouse now that will pay off with compound interest and will help you in the process until God brings you together as husband and wife.

The Power of Prayer

What is one of the most powerful ways you can cultivate your journey to your future spouse? Pray for your future spouse! Do not underestimate the value of praying for your spouse! Your prayers will not return void. I prayed some very specific things for Wladimir years before we ever met and it is amazing to see how God answered those prayers.

Build Your Love Story Now

Think of how you can build you and your spouse's love story now. You can buy little presents and keep them safely stored for your future husband or wife or get them little mementos from places you travel. I met a young woman that collected lingerie pieces for her future honeymoon. You could start a piggy bank using your spare change and reserve it for a future vacation together. Or if you wanted to do something more extravagant you could save cash in a special savings account for an engagement ring or for your future honeymoon or save for the down payment for a home. You could also invest in something valuable for them that can grow over time, like gold or silver. Or here is something that is extremely practical and powerful, if you have debt, pay it off. It will give you amazing freedom entering marriage free from those chains.

Be Creative!

What would be something that would just be super fun for you to be able to surprise your husband or wife with after you are married? Would you like to hand them the keys to the house you bought or give them a bag of silver? Or come walking into the bedroom in a sexy pair of shoes that you bought and saved just for him? Would you like to be able to read to your spouse a journal of prayers that you wrote and prayed over him or her before you ever met? Or maybe write a collection of poems just for your spouse? Or be able to give to him or her a box of letters that you wrote?

Activity 10.7

Do not let where you are at the moment keep you from dreaming!

- 10.7.1. What ideas from the suggestions above would you like to do for your future spouse?

　　_____
　　_____

- 10.7.2. What additional ideas do you have that you could do for them?

　　_____
　　_____

To go deeper on section 10.7
Visit www.ThePowerOfAHoneymoon.com/phmtools

* * *

We Are Built to Have Success in Our Singlehood and Dating

The ideas above may seem far off to you, it might seem impossible to save for a house (I am not saying that you have to buy a house), but if you start in small ways investing into you and your future spouse's love story you will be surprised at the treasure chest you can save along the way. Your spouse will love that you made investments into your marriage and it makes the time waiting for your future spouse more purposeful and fun.

These are the Honeymoon Living leaps to our dating and marriage success that helped us start with-no-hiccups or fits-and-false-starts. The single time in your life is a beautiful season. At times, it can feel like it is full of frustration and heartbreak, but it can also be a time of amazing fulfilling adventure with the Lord packed with fun and expectation. The choice is yours, will you move forward with God in what He is calling you to, or will you choose to go your own way? Just know, that wherever you are in your process, we cheer you on. We highly recommend walking God's path for your life and we say to you that it was worth going through the process of becoming what God was calling us to be as individuals so that we could be what He was calling us to be as a unit. It was worth letting go of the things in the past that held us back, and we can both testify that it was so worth dating God's way. It was worth the wait! We cheer for you in your journey. We believe in you.

To go deeper on this section 10, #SinglehoodAndDatingSuccess
Visit www.ThePowerOfAHoneymoon.com/phmtools

11 HONEYMOON REVOLUTION: MARRIAGE ROADMAP

If you are a Christian and married, you are the panacea to many of the world's problems. You have been particularly equipped with a counterpart for the unique mission God has placed on your life.

The above statement can feel laughable or even mean-spirited if you are currently experiencing a difficult marriage relationship. Though we do not share this message with satire or ill will, we know that you may not feel empowered by our positivity and hope. We do not wish to add any further condemnation or frustration to what you already walk in. Your pain is real.

Your Pain Is Real

We are empathic people, and often without any prompting, people share their stories of hurt and brokenness with us. People talk to us for hours, and most of the time, they feel like they have found a cheerleader in us.

Hearing stories from people close to us who were having real pain in their marriages or dating lives motivated us to find a pathway to successful marriage that would bless us and bless others. If you are reading this book and are someone who has told us your marital pain, your time spent talking to us was not in vain. In this chapter, we will seek to honor God and speak the truth that will bring God's blessing of marriage within your reach.

Some people reading this book will find themselves in urgent situations in their marriage. You think marriage is nearly killing you. If you are in a physical or sexual abuse situation, pick up a phone or go to someone who can help. Please reach out to an abuse support service or emergency service in your community because your safety is worth it. Your life is worth the care immediately.

Others of you are in dangerous situations in which you are contemplating doing harm to yourself or others. Please pick up a phone or go to someone who can help. Please reach out to an emergency service in your community. Doing harm to yourself or another is never justified.

Still others of you are friends to people in the above two scenarios. Please pray for them and reach out to help them in some tangible way.

What is Marriage, Again?

Part of having the revolution in your marriage is to go back to God's original marriage design. God's design for marriage is significant!

The easiest disruption to God's idea of marriage is making or allowing it to be insignificant. In Chapters Three through Six, we addressed the essence of marriage more fully. However, as review, here are a few passages of scripture to restate the key parts of God's design for marriage.

Passage Re-Review: Genesis 1:26, 2:18, 2:24-25

We invite you to peruse The Scriptures, using your Bible or one online. We will use The Amplified® Bible Translation, (AMP). Then we will make a summary observation of the scripture passage verse by verse, which will be labeled "WEJ-Paraphrase."

AMP (Gen. 1:26)

> God said, Let Us [Father, Son, and Holy Spirit] make mankind in Our image, after Our likeness, and let them have complete authority over the fish of the sea, the birds of the air, the [tame] beasts, and over all of the earth, and over everything that creeps upon the earth.
>
> ### WEJ-Paraphrase (Gen. 1:26)

God made humankind patterned after His own image and likeness and based on His attributes as Triune God. None of these qualities is found in the land animals, fishes, or birds. Only Adam received the breath of God (Gen. 2:2). God's spirit lives in humanity and forms them into spiritual beings. Because God gave Adam and Eve His own image, they, too, can create from their choices or will. They are not robots operating without a "free will." Instead, God positioned them with great guidance in the essence of their identity (God's image bearers). God gives nothing without holding the receivers to account. Therefore, God positioned Adam, His image bearer, in the holy garden as a steward. Adam had a choice to live out his God-given abilities to tend the garden, and then to exercise dominion over the animals and the earth.

Summary: God created Adam, and then later completes him with Eve, to perform stewarding tasks in the world; the two have a purpose to fulfill together.

AMP (Gen. 2:18)

Now the Lord God said, it is not good (sufficient, satisfactory) that the man should be alone; I will make him a helper (suitable, adapted, complementary) for him …

WEJ-Paraphrase (Gen. 2:18)

God also created in Adam an external dependency on Eve so that Adam could put into practice the relational and intelligence attributes that God built into him. These are the same attributes displayed in the Triune Godhead of Father and Son and Holy Spirit.

Without another person built for Adam, he would be incomplete forever. Not to mention, Adam could not reproduce by himself.

Summary: Adam and Eve need each other very much.

AMP (Gen. 2:24)

Therefore a man shall leave his father and his mother and shall become united and cleave to his wife, and they shall become one flesh.

WEJ-Paraphrase (Gen. 2:24)

This verse tells us that the story of Adam and Eve is mystically replicated every time a marriage occurs. The same comprehensive joining and dependency happens in every marriage.

<u>Summary</u>: The new couple leaves behind their birth families and is united together as a new family unit; sex consummates their new relationship.

AMP (Gen. 2:25)

And the man and his wife were both naked and were not embarrassed or ashamed in each other's presence. (Gen. 2:25)

WEJ-Paraphrase (Gen. 2:25)

In the verse, the summary description also defines the timeless design of the first and all later marriages. God sets the standard for Adam and Eve to live out the completion of each other (also now known as marriage). God built a marriage to be without the barrier or hindrance of shame and embarrassment between spouses. God, their maker, is an integral part of the union in a spiritual connection and hence no similar barrier (of shame and embarrassment) is permitted between them and God. The spouses are built to have with each other "nakedness" or trust and transparency as their default connection. Second, if the spouses look at themselves from Holy Spirit-filled lenses, they are built to use their spiritual connection between them to encourage one another to embrace the spiritual reality of their completion of each other. They will live together "not ashamed" or without inadequacy issues between each other, which causes them to be in full unity and harmony with one another.

<u>Summary</u>: The couple is enjoying life, sharing everything, and having more sex.

* * *

Debunking the Noisy Distractions to Successful Marriages

God's original blueprint for marriage will never be destroyed, even if our culture tries to redefine marriage through nuances, legalities, or popular opinions. Even though there are legal and civil elements for recognizing and legitimizing marriage in our society, two individuals truly become one in marriage only through God's blueprint and design. Irrespective of human laws and their jurisdiction, the supreme benefits of marriage are only realized through God's design.

It's important to debunk the noisy distractions about what marriage truly is because every experience of a counterfeit marriage results in pain. If people experience the counterfeit instead of the real thing, they may not recognize God's authentic design. It is important to know that God's design of marriage is available to you, and its blessings and benefits are available to you. The pain you are currently experiencing from a counterfeit marriage can be healed by turning towards God's authentic design.

Your Marriage Revolution Roadmap Activities

ACTIVITY INSTRUCTIONS

The rest of this chapter is in an interactive workbook format.

How? We will frequently prompt the readers to pause and observe, answer questions, brainstorm, or invite them to check out external tools to get further help.

Why? FIRST, so you the reader can gain the maximum benefit through participation. **SECOND**, to permit later interactive activities to be-added-on, and accelerate the benefits you gain from the material. **THIRD**, to permit a bridge to have later live interaction with authors and teams dedicated to championing your success in singlehood, marriage, and love by God's design. **FORTH**, as you work through the activities below, you may find yourself wanting to go deeper and explore more.

Additional tools and support at:
www.ThePowerOfAHoneymoon.com/phmtools

Prerequisite Activity 11.1: Sexual Past

- 11.1.1. What was your sexual status upon entering marriage?

  _____
  _____

- 11.1.2. What was your spouse's sexual status upon entering marriage?

  _____
  _____

- 11.1.3. Did you read Chapter 10?

Yes ___ / No ___

If not, we recommend that you review some of the material in Chapter 10, specifically, Part 1: You are Single and Not a Virgin and Part 2: Slay the Dragons of Your Sexual Past. Engaging in those sections from Chapter 10 will especially help you if you struggle with any common sexual, spiritual or emotional roadblocks in your marital intimacy.

Activity 11.1

- 11.1.4. What did you learn from Chapter 10, and did you have to slay any dragons?

  _____
  _____
  _____

Authentic Blueprint Activities:

Activity 11.2

Belief Building Blocks for God's Blueprint

In this section, we will help you clarify the belief building blocks of God's marriage blueprint. God's blessed version of marriage is, "*The two shall become one flesh...never to be pulled apart.*" However, mix and matching different marriage ideas with God's version will cause unnecessary problems and unpredictable results at best. Even an implicit or subconscious mix and match of marriage blueprints creates long-term problems for a Christ-follower.

BEFORE WE START

This is a two-part activity. For each complete the sentence phrases:
(Part 1) circle the option that you believe, "can" or "cannot."
Example: "I believe my marriage *(circle one)* (can / cannot) _(we help fill-in this blank)_ at mine or my spouse's choosing."
(Part 2): Write-in your rationale
Explain *why* you believe this and *how* do you see this fitting into God's blueprint for marriage.

LET'S START

- 11.2.1. I believe my marriage (can / cannot) **end in divorce** at mine or my spouse's choosing.

Why? _____
How? _____

- 11.2.2. I believe my marriage (can / cannot) **have love die (grow out of love)** at mine or my spouse's choosing.

Why? _____
How? _____

- 11.2.3. I believe my marriage (can / cannot) **_run out of affectionate / sexual romance_** at mine or my spouse's choosing.

Why? _____
How? _____

- 11.2.4. I believe my marriage (can / cannot) _____ *(fill in the blank)* at mine or my spouse's choosing.

Why? _____
How? _____

To go deeper on section 11.2,
  Visit www.ThePowerOfAHoneymoon.com/phmtools

Activity 11.3

Belief Building Blocks for God's Blueprint: Roles of Husband and Wife

- 11.3.1. Explain **_what_** you believe the role of a **husband** is. Explain **_why_** you believe this and **_how_** you see this fitting into God's blueprint for marriage.

What? _____
Why? _____
How? _____

- 11.3.2. Explain **_what_** you believe the role of a **wife** is. Explain **_why_** you believe this and **_how_** you see this fitting into God's blueprint for marriage.

What? _____
Why? _____
How? _____

To go deeper on section 11.3,
  Visit www.ThePowerOfAHoneymoon.com/phmtools

Activity 11.4

Belief Building Blocks for God's Blueprint: Calling as a Marital Unit

Every believer is placed on earth by God to fulfill a purpose. Those who are married have a unique, joint purpose to fulfill with their spouse. Your union has a special calling God has given to you, but if you ignore your joint purpose, you will likely have a sense of unfulfillment because you are not fully living according to God's blueprint for your marriage (Gen. 1:26).

- 11.4.1. *What* do you think you and your spouse's unique calling is?

_____
_____
_____

- 11.4.2. *Why* do you believe this?

_____
_____
_____

- 11.4.3. *How* do you see this fitting into God's blueprint for marriage?

_____
_____
_____

- 11.4.4. *How* did God confirm this to you as a couple?

_____
_____
_____

If you are not sure what your unique calling as a couple is, start by thinking through what both you and your spouse mutually have a heart for. What do you both enjoy? What do you both dislike? What do you want to see changed in the world? If you do not know what your unique call as a couple is, start by filling in the above exercise with what you think it might be and ask God to reveal it to you.

To go deeper on section 11.4,
   Visit www.ThePowerOfAHoneymoon.com/phmtools

Activity 11.5

Pass on God's Blueprint for Marriage to Others Through a Marriage That Inspires.

Every believer, individually and especially those with a spouse have the opportunity and privilege to represent God's authentic marriage blueprint well. A Christian marriage that does not inspire others falls short of God design for marriage. *One caveat is using the categories, which God will judge by, and not random arbitrary categories that God does not judge by or is contradictory to His blueprint.*

BEFORE WE START

STEP 1: Circle from two sets of options to complete the sentence.

Option set one, circle from the option that you believe, "**is inspiring**" or "**is uninspiring.**"

Option set two, circle the option that you believe, "**the evidence**" or "**the missing evidence.**"

STEP 2: Fill in the blank with an answer from the List A (In List A are *activities prioritized in the authentic marriage blueprint*

List A

1. Our Unity (i.e., how the noticeable harmony / oneness between spouse is demonstrated?)
2. Our Impact (i.e., how the purpose / calling of the marriage is demonstrated?)

3. Our Loving care and affection (i.e., how the agape and passion for each other is demonstrated?)

4. (Fill in the blank) _____

Example:

I believe our marriage (*is inspiring / is uninspiring*) to **our children** *(applicable if you are parents)* because of comments or feedback made by them about (*the evidence / the missing evidence*) of (*chosen from List A*) <u>Our Unity</u>.

LET'S START

- 11.5.1. I believe our marriage (*is inspiring / is uninspiring*) to **our children** *(applicable if you are parents)* because of comments or feedback made by them about (*the evidence / the missing evidence*) of <u>our</u> (*choose from List A*) _____.

- 11.5.2. I believe our marriage (*is inspiring / is uninspiring*) to **our community** because of comments or feedback made by them about (*the evidence / the missing evidence*) of <u>our</u> (*choose from List A*) _____.

- 11.5.3. I believe our marriage (*is inspiring / is uninspiring*) to **our** fill-in blank _____ because of comments or feedback made by them about (*the evidence / the missing evidence*) of <u>our</u> (*choose from List A*) _____.

To go deeper on section 11.5,
  Visit www.ThePowerOfAHoneymoon.com/phmtools

* * *

Getting Back to Basics

In Chapter 4, we talked about the one enemy that exists in your marriage and in your life. Remember that this enemy is not all-powerful, but is already terminally defeated, and has been served a sentence of judgment and destruction. Furthermore, Jesus will beat him out of your marriage, every day, if you defer to the Holy Spirit. Every failing or challenge in your marriage is from an undetected lie the enemy once told to one or both spouses. You *must* kill the lie and any offshoot of it from the deceiving enemy, the devil. Just as the perfect couple Adam and Eve was a perfect match, but then got unraveled, *so can your marriage be with your perfect match* and yet face steep opposition from the enemy especially if you don't undo in your marriage any and every existing lie against God's design of marriage.

One day at a time, you can beat back the enemy. We cannot shorten the enemy's long-term fate to his destruction so he would stop lobbing tempting deceptive lies at us. However, because of Jesus, the enemy incurs defeat daily from those husbands and wives who depend on Jesus and the Holy Spirit for their marriage success. You have been given the advantage!

The above activities were created to help you align your beliefs with God's blueprint and to determine if there are any distractions in your way. Once your focus is diverted from God, soon it will be diverted from other parts of your marriage, too. What happened when Adam and Eve diverted their focus from God? They had a polite conversation with the serpent, and the serpent deceived them with a twisted way to think about God (then Adam and Eve chose to take their focus off God in the process).

This chapter focused on *uprooting your one enemy*, the already-defeated foe of God, from your focus. Getting this enemy off your shoulders and out of your life was the task in this chapter. The enemy against your marriage is actually against God your Creator. Hence, the enemy tries to distract you with his deceptive antics—a million and more little ways to accomplish his one main goal of distracting you from God even just a little.

11 HONEYMOON REVOLUTION: MARRIAGE ROADMAP

Your relationship with God will be the source of any truly enduring good you receive while on earth and will be the answer to any difficulty you will have to overcome. First love for God is the only answer to having a first love for your spouse. Everything else will lead to a twisted reality, no matter how good a thing it is. The above activities were meant to give you a baseline for where you stand today and to be used as a reference point for future action.

Examples of Critical Activities that Blossom the Authentic Marriage

1. Keep Spiritual Disciplines Intact: Scripture Reading, Prayer, Fasting, Regularly using God's gift both directly and indirectly at God's work (live out your discipleship).
2. Example of spiritual disciplines in action: Reading the Bible in 90-days, or 1-year; Journaling your prayers; Praying together aloud to each other; Going on spiritual retreats together.
3. Listen to God's daily and frequent guidance for yourself, your marriage, and your marital role (live out your discipleship).
4. Stay in constant forgiveness, love, and mercy toward yourself and your spouse (through agape love).

The above activities produce deep heart-connectedness between the spouses, which then creates free-flowing emotional, spiritual, physical intimacy, and passion.

Once Basics Are In Place, If More Help Is Needed, Try This—"Re-Do It"

If your marriage is not working, you may need to have your honeymoon or marriage "re-done."

There are two prerequisites for re-doing your honeymoon or marriage. First, take the Praying for Your Spouse Challenge (more info below). Then, study and familiarize yourself with the authentic marriage blueprint based on Genesis 1–3, Ephesians 5, 1 Corinthians 13, Revelations 2:1-7, and the life of Jesus in the Gospels. Understanding the life of Jesus is critical to living a marriage according to God's authentic blueprint for marriage.

Details of the Praying for Your Spouse Challenge:

> **How long are we doing this?** Fourteen days and then reflect on the events.
>
> **What do I need?** *The Power of a Praying® Husband Book of Prayers* (ISBN 9780736957632 (pbk) 9780736957649 (ebook), *The Power of a Praying® Wife Book of Prayers* (ISBN 9780736957519 (pbk) or 9780736957526 (ebook); The *Pocketbook Prayer Books* are by Stormie Omartian. (Find these at your local bookstore or visit www.ThePowerOfAHoneymoon.com/tools/spousechallenge).
>
> **How do I start?** Take the Spouse Challenge Survey before you begin (*Visit* www.ThePowerOfAHoneymoon.com/spousechallenge).
>
> This survey will help you create a baseline in your journey. After the fourteen-day is done, on the fifteen-day, come back and take the Spouse Challenge Survey again.
>
> **What do I do?** Pray through your prayer book for your spouse and expect God to radically show up and show off in your prayer time and marriage. Aim toward praying through the whole book each day. If your spouse is not interested in accompanying you on this journey, it is okay. Simply go pray!

To go deeper on this section 11, #SpouseChallenge
Visit www.ThePowerOfAHoneymoon.com/phmtools

Honeymoon Re-Do

If you had a lackluster honeymoon, and then add another honeymoon vacation to your calendar. Arrange a nice vacation destination, but be sure that the amenities or settings don't conflict with prioritizing each other. Being together is your only agenda item. If you decide to engage in a few outside activities, choose ones that allow you to learn something new together, that teach you about each other, and that help you grow in your ability to perform a joint task better, like dance lessons, a couples cooking class, etc.

Wedding Re-Do

You may have to abandon the first wedding ceremony you experienced together, especially if it was a hoax of a wedding or just some kind of a legal arrangement. Is God telling you that the first ceremony wasn't enough to move you into a honeymoon living marriage? Do you need to re-do your wedding in order to move forward in your marriage?

Begin your RE-DO wedding with new vows. If possible, write your own custom vows, vows that you will be inspired by every day and that are based on the authentic blueprint. Afterwards, go on an excellent honeymoon.

We Are Built to Have Success in Love and Our Marriage

As Christians, we are built with one spiritual heart from which to be loving and do loving things to God, and others, starting with our spouse, our children and then all people. For example, God intends as bride and groom, the loving heart we experienced during our wonderful honeymoon time away to be the same heart to love one another throughout our lifetime until death or glory-do-us-two-part. God gives the spouses each only one spiritual heart from which to love.

We don't have advice from God's loving guidance in Scripture to have a divided heart, a heart for our kids more precious and loving than a heart for our spouse, or a different heart for loving our Lord than for loving our spouse. We have advice from God's Scripture that we have been built to be naked, trusting and sincere with God; and the practice we perfect with God will guide us on how to be naked with our spouse, and agape loving with our children. Lastly, the overflow from receiving God's love and wholeheartedly loving God back will enable us selflessly to bring God's love to the hurts God sees in the world.

We are built to love from God's overflow of love to us, and from us back to Him, the cure to idolatry. Idolatry is somewhat the attempt to fill our

God-built-love-tank without walking in nakedness, and in an active alive loving trusting relationship with God. Then out of our discernible love dehydration, we ill-advisedly increase our effort at searching for the biggest and best counterfeit love fuel, our possession in our X, Y, and Z; the enemy lies and whispers differently for every person, e.g., mansion, beautiful mate, affluence, etc. Success at love and life from God design is much easier and spiritually coherent, efficient and life-giving. God built us to function simply with His one wonderful blueprint, love Him first and foremost, and He will take care of the rest.

Feel free to invite our guidance in rediscovering the authentic blueprint. We will do our best to connect and help. Additionally, if you would like special prayers, please contact us. Prayer changes things, and we will pray.

Daily we pray for Christian marriages, (and singles, who are called to marriage in their future) who are in our local community and the seven continents. Hence, marriages around the world are being prayed for by others and us because we love you and are cheering for God's blessings on His marriage creation to be resilient from enemy attacks. We invite you to join us in praying for marriages, even if your marriage is facing a challenge in the moment. Together through the spiritual force of prayer in your community and around the world, we will improve and inspire love, and marriage from God's design.

The next chapter takes us to the tremendous beginning of a marriage, the wedding day celebration and shows us why to celebrate marriage.

12 HOPE IN A HONEYMOON MARRIAGE REVOLUTION

The ceremony was set for December 13, 2014, at 4 o'clock in the afternoon. When the day arrived, we were sure of only one thing: we would get married. It just seemed that the end of the earth was not going to happen that day. Nothing short of the world ending would have kept us from getting married that day. Then we truly entered into the day, and began the second part the authentic marriage blueprint, the *leave and cleave* at the wedding event, discussed in this chapter.

Elyssa, a virgin bride, had saved her first kiss for our wedding day and had spent her life focused on and motivated for this day. I, as a first-time groom and spiritually rededicated virgin, had only recently figured out the beauty of marriage, and seen that it was probably God's greatest creation. Once I understood the holiness of marriage, I had deep gratitude for it and for God giving it to me.

Leading up to the day, we didn't exactly know how it would unfold. We had been fervently praying for the wedding day to be a genuine blessing, and not only to us. We prayed it would be filled with the wonder of God as we entered into His holy and heavenly plan for us. When I awoke that morning, I knew we were embarking on something that was unique, but not necessarily divine. Who would have known? We were about to experience the final part of God's authentic marriage blueprint as He joined us together just like Adam and Eve so long ago. After our one-year-plus of pursuing God together, our honorable dating season was now leading into a divine promotion, where God intervened, making two single lives into one flesh.

The Wedding Day in Action

It was a day of wrecks: five times that day, heaven collided with our wedding event. God was working in our lives as we finalized entrance into His authentic marriage blueprint and, at best, we could respond with profound gratitude. None of our study and preparation for marriage could have prepared us for the heavenly collisions that took place on our wedding day.

> "*21And the Lord God caused a deep sleep to fall upon Adam; and while he slept, He took one of his ribs or a part of his side and closed up the [place with] flesh. 22And the rib or part of his side which the Lord God had taken from the man He built up and made into a woman, and He brought her to the man. 23Then Adam said, This [creature] is now bone of my bones and flesh of my flesh; she shall be called Woman, because she was taken out of a man. 24Therefore a **man shall leave his father and his mother** and **shall become united and cleave to his wife**, and they shall become one flesh.*" Genesis 2:21-24, AMP

Wrecks

Wreck One – The Reveal

The first wreck happened just before the reveal, a time set aside for the first gaze between the groom and beautiful bride. As the groom, I had made peace with God; nothing from my past was unresolved or lacking closure. There was no shame, remorse, or concern leading up to this day. But as I stood on the other side of the door, it was as if I was transported back to the Garden of Eden. At that moment, I had become Adam, incomplete on my own, waiting for my completion by my bride. Suddenly, I was a wreck, singing aloud—praising God and crying uncontrollably at the miraculous act of joining us together that was happening now. It seemed that just as he had joined Adam and Eve, he was joining us together, Wladimir and Elyssa.

I praised God's goodness with all I had while I waited on the steps for my Eve, Elyssa. During the divine joining, God permitted me to get a true glimpse of my incompletion without His suitable helpmate Elyssa. I was leaving my previously held completion identity or status in God willingly and fully. In exchange, I was gladly cleaving to the new completion identity God gave me in joining me to my suitable helpmate Elyssa. God was crashing into our world, and I thanked Him for it. Then, the door opened, and the voice of the wedding planner said, "You can now see your bride." And there she was: my Eve, my completion, and there was more cause for thanksgiving to God.

Wreck Two – The Praise

We, as a collective community, provoked the second collision; we couldn't help it! The ceremony was moving nicely. After the homily and communion, we transitioned to a time of prayer led by our parents and a few other important people in our lives.

However, before our prayers started, the thanksgiving praises seemed to connect sharply with heaven. But why? Not because of how loudly we uttered our thanksgivings. It was because our thanksgiving praises were deeply sincere, since we were all struck by the dreamlike moment we were witnessing.

God had handsomely rewarded the community and us after many years. There were likely 38-plus years of prayers invested by our parents and the community on our behalf. Their prayers over scores of years were the main factor in Elyssa and me heartily arriving on that day. Their prayers helped us individually to overcome life's hardships (which could have made this day irrelevant). They helped us, uniquely, to be each other's suitable match, and to date honorably. Lastly, they helped us to marry in a fashion that honored them and God. No wonder we were motivated with one accord to seek out God in heaven and to deliver our gratitude to Him. We were so thankful to the giver of all good gifts, and these grateful hearts produced unusual honor and praise to God at our wedding.

Wreck Three – Parental and Community Prayer Send-Off

The community was getting good at instigating the collisions, and they once again went for it. During the group prayer segment of our ceremony, our parents and several members of the Christian community prayed wonder-filled blessings over us. They commissioned us with various prayers, for example,

"Lord, they have already been your light to hundreds of thousands of people across the world; now as they become one, let them champion your call of marriage globally."

"Lord, people say that honeymoons end, but they don't have to. Let them live honeymoon love their entire life."

"Lord, please make them a husband and wife of prayer."

The prayers were full of bold declarations over who we would be as a couple. In their prayers, they fulfilled their parental and community obligation to ignite powerfully "*leave his father and his mother*," releasing us from past social or familial obligations and expectations on us as singles. Then, spurring us forward to unite and cleave together around our future calling, "*he shall become united to his wife and cleave to his wife.*" Heaven didn't remain silent, but responded, affirming that those were good prayers to pray. God was affirming that we were praying the right things. It felt as though heaven reached down and declared on earth to us who we were called to be and equipped our marriage for that calling at that moment. It was an exalted time, and the presence of God was palpable.

Wreck Four – Ties Shattered

My mom instigated the fourth collision as she prayed for us, but God fired right back. She thanked God immensely for her seeing this day of her son getting married honorably. She acknowledged that my life had been hard; growing up without parents and then my birth father dying by the time I was 23. As she spoke, I sensed her gratitude for the wedding day, but also her past pain. She was prevented from being the bride and mother she was called to be. A Christ-filled Ephesians 5 husband had not nourished her. As her prayers and praises intermingled, tears welled up in my eyes and heart. I felt my gentle mother's pain; I grieved for the father I never had in my dad, the Christ-husband my father was not, but could have been. More tears. I had never cried for this before. I felt pain for my mother as I had never before felt for her. I was filled with tears and sadness, yet not out of pity and sentimentalism.

Then God showed up with utter clarity to guide me to my future marriage calling. He clarified that these events from the past, which had caused such pain, were from the enemy to do further hurt to me. The enemy meant to make me cleave to my past pain and make it an obstacle to me as a future husband and father. Instead, God would galvanize me to cleave to a future opposite to my parents' past. While the past could have been a hindrance, now the Holy Spirit was using it to give a clarion call and unction to be a champion Christian husband for my bride Elyssa and a godly Christian father for our future children. God would transform the ashes of my mother's pain into a rose-wrapped letter from God. He commissioned me to be a groom like Christ to my bride Elyssa.

When Christ crashes into our existence out of the ashes of the past, God will raise up a new generation. Generational spiritual curses and pain can be severed instantly and prevented from going any further.

Wreck Five – Take Hold

As the groom, I received multiple commissions from the prayers that were prayed during our wedding. God's hand in my mom's commission was immediately noticeable, but I did not recognize the significance of some of the others until about a month later. As Elyssa and I watched the ceremony on video, I was blown away by how particular prayers prayed at our wedding had already found root and fruit in our marriage. For instance, someone prayed that I would be a husband of prayer. That became a reality in my life, not because I am so pious and was looking to add to my piety, but because of the prayer on my wedding day. This prayer found root and created fruit in our marriage, and life will never be the same.

Someone else prayed during the wedding commission that our honeymoon would never end. We are living out that reality. This book is tangible evidence of the commission at our wedding to live out the authentic marriage blueprint of God.

There is power in the wedding ceremonies of authentic marriages, because the Christian community is present along with God to transport the couple into their marriage covenant. The community as a whole benefits, along with the couple, from a wedding ceremony that honors God and His creation of marriage. They all benefit by witnessing Christians exercising their spiritual gifts among one another for the greater good of the community.

This statement is not a slam against the justice of the peace, a drive-up wedding booth, or an elopement. Perhaps if the engaged couple were to approach their wedding at those places with total honor to the Lord and marriage, then God's special heavenly collision and blessing might come on the wedding day. But, if done without awe and wonder at God's dating and marriage blueprint, then the divine heavenly collision on the wedding day is forfeited. It seems there are two significant keys to God's wedding day collision and visitation: the bride and groom honor God with their life, and the inner-circle community and parents (or those filling-in) similarly reverence and celebrate God and marriage.

A Panacea to the World's Ills

Many hungry communities could be fed and clothed by dollars that instead are spent on costly divorce proceedings. In the United States alone, divorce is a $28 billion-a-year industry, with the average divorce costing $15,000 (source: www.divorcestatistics.info/how-much-does-divorce-cost-in-the-usa.html).

A marriage based on God's authentic blueprint for marriage cannot end in divorce; hence, more marriages born or transformed into authentic marriages according to the original covenant of Adam and Eve will save money and relieve stress for the couple, their family and the world. Instead of investing in the dissolution of their marriage, couples can instead follow God's blueprint for marriage and choose to dedicate their money and time to the needs of their community or the world.

What if more couples experienced the authentic marriage blueprint? There would be more first-time authors like us or repeat authors and co-authors freed from the time-consuming distraction of disharmony in their marriages and able to invest their creative energy into unlimited possibilities. How many more artists, musicians, songwriters (with more songs of agape-love written from experience), new professions, and inventions would there be if couples grabbed ahold of world-changing commissions and then went forth and lived out those commissions for the authentic purposes of their marriages?

The Christian wedding at its best is a celebration of God, and expectation to experience and receive God's spiritual acts intertwined with human events. Marriage is one magnificent creation of God, so is entrepreneurship and the church community. As more marriages are lived at God's standard and agape-fuel, the other institutions will be that much more revolutionized by the revolutionary couples. Revolutionary Christ-centered weddings allow the bride and groom to break from the baggage of past generations and be catapulted into the future. The couple must continue daily trusting God and walking out a-first-love for their spouses and God. However, the wedding day event is a significant start, and reaffirms and passes on our Christian faith and God's blueprint for marriage.

The Richness of a Wedding for Singles

Our wedding day was truly one of the most glorious days of our lives. It was the culmination of many hopes and dreams and proof of God's hand of restoration. The two of us, as well as those in attendance, reveled at the magnitude of what God had done and what He launched on that day. Look what God had done. He had taken two people from wildly different upbringings, on very different journeys, with different strengths and talents and called them to be one. Our wedding day seemed like magic, but it was just normal according to the authentic design for dating with purity and marriage built on God's blueprint. Our wedding was a springboard into a powerful marriage, a momentous occasion that—especially if you are not married, please know this—was worth the wait. It was worth battling temptations to compromise; it was worth fighting to maintain God's definition of purity.

The Richness of a Wedding for the Community Present

Every person attending the wedding can have the same passion for marriage. They can contribute to the ceremony by conferring and commissioning the groom and bride in faith. Christian parents also can play a significant role in the wedding as God's vehicle for sending off their children into the future with spiritual blessings passed from generation to generation. As well, they can be the ones to obliterate the spiritual curses of past generations and prevent them from being passed on to the next generation. Finally, parents can cast vision and help catapult their children into the unique calling God has for them as a couple, a calling often discernible even on the wedding day.

It Is Time for a Revolution

Are we overstating the importance of an authentic Christian marriage? Can the dating and marriage relationship built on God's authentic blueprint be right and every other experience of dating and marriage be wrong?

Martin Luther, facing similar odds, said: "I cannot and will not recant anything, for to go against conscience is neither right nor safe. Here I stand, I can do no other, so help me God. Amen."

We will believe the impossible with you and for you, hoping you will invite us to walk alongside you.

Believe for "The Impossible"

It is time to believe God radically. It's time to believe the impossible is possible and to seek God's face for His strategies for our relationships. His heart's desire is that we would experience the fullness of what He has for our lives and the fullness of His plan for marriage. We are cheering for you and will fight for you in your journey. As we wrap up, we pray this prayer charge over you. We encourage you to read it aloud for yourself and make it a declaration over your life, your marriage, and your future. It is not a flippant prayer that we pray for you, on the contrary, we pound heaven's door for you.

> *Lord God Almighty, right now, we lift up to You every shattered heart, every broken marriage, and every impossible marriage situation. We ask, Father, that your peace would come upon each person in desperate need of a breakthrough. Lord, in Matthew 21:21, your word says that we can speak to the mountains, and they shall be moved, so we speak to those mountains to be moved right now. We speak to every couple in disunity, we speak to every spouse who is cheating in thought or action, and we ask your Holy Spirit to blow over each one of those circumstances and move them. Let their hearts be wrecked with conviction and repentance. Let there be a mighty wave of restoration that crashes upon those marriages. We speak to every lost spouse, every spouse who does not claim You as their Lord and Savior, and we ask You to move them. We bind up the lies of the enemy and ask that he (the already-defeated enemy) would fall into his own traps. We liberate your truth into the lives of those who don't know You and ask that their hearts would be softened by the extravagant love their spouse has shown them. We ask for the transformation of their lives that they would radically abandon themselves to You and invite You into their lives as their Lord, Savior, and first love.*
>
> *We speak to every person reading this who does not know You, or who is struggling in their relationship with You, or who needs an*

increasing desire to know You; move them, Father. We ask that they would answer your call and invite You to be the Lord and Savior of their lives, saying, "Lord, I need You. I need your guidance and help. Please wash me of my sins, remove every filthy thing from my life, burn out of me whatever You need to remove. I release control of my life to You. I invite You, Jesus Christ, to be the Lord and Savior of my life in a fresh way, in a deeper way. I invite your Holy Spirit to fill me now."

We speak to every broken heart, every heart that is crushed, move them with life and bring healing to them. We declare hope and healing on their souls that they would be filled supernaturally with the restoration of the Holy Spirit. We speak to every situation and heart that needs restoring, every marriage that needs healing, and every need, spoken and unspoken, that needs filling, and invite your Holy Spirt to do a mighty work in those places. We bless every couple and every person who has a desire to see their marriage grow in unity, connectedness, honor, fun, and passion. We declare the fullness of what You intended for marriage to take place in their lives and marriage. Wherever there are any roots of doubt or hidden issues that would suppress the growth of honeymoon love, we ask You to uproot them. We agree and declare the growth of ever-increasing honeymoon love over your marriage or future marriage.

We bless all the single people reading this book, Lord. You know every desire of their hearts, You know every struggle, You know the tears they have cried, and You know exactly where they are. Singles (and married folks, whatever applies to you, you can receive, too), we bless you from the top of your head to the bottom of your feet. We declare restoration over you. We declare the fullness of God's promises over your life. We ask God to encompass you radically with His power. We declare a supernatural growth of faith over you. We attack by the power of the blood of the Lamb every spirit that would attack or hold you back from living fully in the power that God designed

12 HOPE IN A HONEYMOON MARRIAGE REVOLUTION

you to live in. We ask the Holy Spirit to come and fill those places now. We impart the gift of purity to you. We declare over you a rededication of purity and spiritual (and even physical) restoration of virginity. We declare over you endurance with grace and ease. We pray for your future spouses, that God would do in them what He needs to accomplish and that He would bring you together in His perfect timing. We combat unneeded delays and heartbreaks; we pray against discouragement that would attack you. We declare the hope and truth of heaven over you. We pray that you would burn with desire for a powerful indwelling of the Holy Spirit.

Receive the blessings of the Lord, and walk forth in power and unity with the Spirit of God. Heaven blesses you and declares over you that you are not forgotten. The King of kings chooses you. He holds you, and He is faithful to His promises and will complete the good work that He started in you.

We seal this prayer with the blood of Jesus of Christ. Amen.

We believe in you! We cheer you on! We pray for you frequently. We invite you to continue with us on your journey. In addition, if you have not already done so, join us at www.WladimirAndElyssa.com. We would love you to connect with us and share your story with us! We also answer questions, post new content, provide additional resources, schedule consultations, book speaking engagements, as well as offer discounted bulk ordering options if you want to share The Power Of A HONEYMOON™ Marriage book with your friends, family, group study, or church or school bookstore. Contact us at www.WladimirAndElyssa.com for more information.

You have now been dubbed an ambassador of the Honeymoon Marriage Revolution. Together let us live it, one moment at a time.
Wladimir and Elyssa Joseph

About the Author

One day I texted my beloved bride, Elyssa, three new nicknames that came to mind for us as a couple. Of the three, she picked the nickname "Marriage Pit Bulls." Though we had vastly different upbringings, in hindsight we discovered that we created our own revolutionary journey through singlehood and dating, to get to our glorious promotion to marriage. Not many women make it to their wedding day as virgin brides at 32 years old, and not many spiritually rededicated virgin grooms lead the way in waiting for a first kiss at the wedding altar.

Elyssa comes from a deep Christian family heritage and has been hands-on involved in Christian ministry, training, and leadership for over 25 years. Wladimir has roots spiritually grounded from the Brooklyn Tabernacle Church and a master's degree from Trinity Evangelical Divinity School, with emphasis on Theology and Christian Counseling.

From our observations from 70 combined years of being single and as astute bystanders, we see that many marriages are being severely attacked. We were on guard when facing dating, love, and marriage. We know that the barriers we overcame along the path to our glorious marriage are the same ones we are called to help others overcome.

When you are ready to pursue married, dating, or single living from a successful, authentic blueprint, contact us. We care about these things with a pit-bull–like tenacity and a heightened alarm at the obstacles to love according to God's design. Let's connect soon!

www.WladimirAndElyssa.com / Email: Honeymoon@wladimirandelyssa.com / Twitter: @elyssa_wladimir / www.Facebook.com/elyssaandwladimir / plus.google.com/u/0/ElyssaAndWladimirJosephLive/posts

www.ingramcontent.com/pod-product-compliance
Lightning Source LLC
LaVergne TN
LVHW051557070426
835507LV00021B/2616